"People who write leadership books need to first lead in some significant setting. Linda Clark has done that—making a profound difference training women's ministry leaders across the United States. Over the years, she's received hundreds of questions about women's ministry. Linda has compiled her answers in this practical guide to answer your real-life questions about women's ministry. Read it, apply it, and increase your effectiveness as a leader."

—JEFF IORG, president, Gateway Seminary

"In *Around the Table: Practical Advice for Effective Women Leaders*, Linda Clark offers useful and timely advice for women in leadership. As Linda shares from her own experiences, readers will feel as if they are sitting down, having a cup of coffee, and discussing some of the top issues that women in leadership face. They will be encouraged and equipped to lead in a godly and effective way in whatever leadership role they may find themselves."

—ALLISON KINION, director of women's missions and ministry, State Convention of Baptists in Indiana

"*Around the Table* reveals a long-time leader's great passion for encouraging and equipping other leaders. Linda writes conversationally and clearly; and the question-and-answer format flows well. There is much practical advice in *Around the Table*—it will be a helpful resource for every woman's leadership library."

—GARY YOCHUM, ministry coordinator, Southeastern Indiana Baptist Association

"Once again Dr. Clark has produced a resource that makes her the master of practical. Every word guides the reader to the essentials of being a godly leader in their home, place of employment, church, and community. Clark guides the reader into better leadership out of her own life-long journey as a leader in her own home and world of employment. Reinforcing the text, Dr. Clark provides an appendix of multiple practical checklists and guides, enabling individualized application of newfound leadership principles. *Around the Table* helps meet the call for men and women to be biblical leaders in our world today."

—MICHAEL B. MCCULLOUGH, interim executive director, California Southern Baptist Convention

Around the Table

OTHER NEW HOPE® BOOKS BY
Dr. Linda M. Clark

5 Leadership Essentials for Women:
Developing Your Ability to Make Things Happen

Found Treasures:
Discovering Your Worth in Unexpected Places

Awaken the Leader in You:
10 Life Essentials for Women in Leadership

PRACTICAL ADVICE FOR
EFFECTIVE WOMEN LEADERS

◆

Around the Table

DR. LINDA M. CLARK

NEW HOPE®
PUBLISHERS
Gospel-Centered. Missions-Driven.

BIRMINGHAM, ALABAMA

New Hope® Publishers
PO Box 12065
Birmingham, AL 35202-2065
NewHopePublishers.com
New Hope Publishers is a division of WMU®.

Library of Congress Cataloging-in-Publication Data

Names: Clark, Linda, 1944- author.
Title: Around the table : practical advice for effective women leaders / Linda M. Clark.
Description: First [edition]. | Birmingham : New Hope Publishers, 2017.
Identifiers: LCCN 2017012768 | ISBN 9781625915290 (permabind)
Subjects: LCSH: Christian women. | Leadership in women. | Leadership--Religious aspects--Christianity.
Classification: LCC BV4527 .C545 2017 | DDC 248.8/43--dc23
LC record available at https://lccn.loc.gov/2017012768

ISBN-13: 978-1-62591-529-0

N184103 • 0717 • 2.5M1

DEDICATION

This book is dedicated to my former leadership team in California. They were ready to learn, passionate about their work, enthusiastic, and committed to excellence under the guidance of Jesus Christ. It was great to serve with you gals!

CONTENTS

APPENDIX

ACKNOWLEDGMENTS

I could never have completed this book without the supportive help (and suggestions) of my husband, Jan. You're one of a kind, sweetie!

INTRODUCTION

Around the Table was born from the multitude of conversations I had with women after making presentations about leadership and its challenges. Its content emerged from whispered comments such as, "I'd like to find a leader like her!"; "Why can't our women's group keep leaders?"; "I just don't have time to do things the way I know they should be done"; "I enlist leaders; I train them, and then in six months, they're gone! What am I doing wrong?"; and, "I'm just so tired; I don't think I can handle another year of the same old thing!"

I've led conferences, coordinated leadership training events, met with large and small groups about leadership, and had one-on-one meetings. Leadership is a complicated subject! Our minds think about skill sets, techniques, approaches, and strategies. Then we start thinking about personalities, schedules, and balancing issues. As if that isn't enough, financial challenges rear their ugly heads, and then we are mired in calendar dates and scheduling conflicts. About the time all of these things crowd in on us and we are at our lowest, our families or spouses ask, "Why are you gone all the time? When will this madness stop? You look tired—what's wrong?"

Unfortunately, such is a leader's life much of the time. I began to think that it might help leaders to know there are other women who feel the same way. Perhaps a discussion about some of the issues with possible solutions would alleviate the stress and frustration. So, I developed a women's leadership survey, and as I traveled for my job, I asked women in all types of leadership roles to pretend they were talking to a well-known and successful leader. What two questions would they ask her?

With more than 175 surveys in hand, I began to sift through them and categorize their questions for easy reference. When the same questions were asked again and again, I knew those issues were of great importance. The responses to my survey came from women of all ages and various educational and cultural backgrounds. Some were married; others were single. Knowing the answers to the questions they asked would be helpful as they served as volunteers, entrepreneurs, supervisors, stay-at-home moms, and community leaders. And nearly all the questions fell into a few specific categories.

Those categories I curated from the survey became the table of contents of this book. What a journey researching those questions and writing this book has been! Reading what others have said about balance, motivation, communication, a woman's call, priorities, and training was an invigorating experience. I don't propose to have all the answers, but with help from some experts, I'm hoping you'll be encouraged and will grow in your leadership skills. My purpose is to provide an easy reference tool you can use from time to time as different situations arise.

We all like success stories, don't we? Well, here's one for you:

It's strange, but I can't remember where I first met her. She and her husband worked within our state, equipping leaders and encouraging pastors. We attended a conference, and during a break, he mentioned to me that he thought his wife would be interested in working with women in missions. That was music to my ears, and I contacted her as soon as I got home. She and I began to meet regularly to see how she would fit into our women's team. She became one of our consultants, and we worked together for more than eight years. She was innovative, faithful, and eager to lead other women to participate in missions.

She had a lot of questions, and we spent hours developing a strategy for involving women and their churches in missions-related activities. She became a strong, stable leader. Why? One reason was because she wasn't timid about asking questions! When she became involved in a national emphasis, she had many questions about process and purpose. Time passed, and my friend felt God calling her to further her education by earning a master's degree in ministry. She asked me to be one of her field mentors. We met at a coffee shop near both our homes and spent more time investigating how she could fine-tune her leadership skills and engage new women in ministry. She participated in a prayer group, met with pastors' wives, and formed relationships that helped her grow spiritually as well as educationally. She is able to do much of what she does because she asked questions.

Successful leaders have stories to tell, and those stories develop because leaders ask questions. You can do the same thing! I believe this book will answer many of your questions about leadership. Chapter 1 features testimonies of women leaders, and chapter 2 contains two brief Bible studies from Ecclesiastes and Proverbs that provide a biblical basis for the discussions that follow. Questions from the women's leadership surveys are arranged in eight additional chapters, and the final chapter is a compilation of questions I answer from my own personal experiences. The appendices provide a reading list and ideas for using the book in small-group and retreat settings. For quick reference or in a time of a leadership emergency, use the subject guide to locate a specific topic!

Enjoy!

CHAPTER 1

◆

No Small Courage: Testimonies of Women in Leadership

The women in this chapter represent the past and present. They are different ages and are ethnically diverse. My hope is their experiences will help you understand that you too can be a strong leader and impact others' lives in your workplace, church, family, and even the world.

I've chosen these women because they embody qualities I aspire to. Some I have only read about while others I've been fortunate enough to work with and interview about their leadership roles. If you were to sit down and talk with them, these are the stories they would tell.

A TRUE RISK-TAKER

Pandita Ramabai lived from 1858–1922 and has the distinction of being the only woman to have translated the entire Bible. Contrary to Hindu practices of the day, Pandita's father believed women should be educated. By the time she was 12 years old, she had memorized 18,000 Sanskrit verses. After losing both her parents at a young age, Pandita and her brother traveled throughout India. When she heard about Christianity, she compared the Bible with Hindu scriptures and saw a stark contrast between Hindu's low opinion of women and the Bible's high value of all life. Visits to England and the United States provided more evidence that the Hindu way of life was not the only way of life.

After coming to know Christ as her personal Savior in 1891, Pandita began a crusade for improved treatment of Indian females. Through the years, she opened schools for widows, orphans, and abandoned babies. She helped women set up bazaars to sell crafts and established skills training programs for them. She even taught girls how to set type and run a printing press. When a famine struck in 1896, Pandita traveled around India and gathered hundreds of starving widows and children and took them to a mission she'd established. Hundreds converted to Christianity because of her witness. She translated the Bible into the Indian language Mahrathi during the last 15 years of her life. When she became extremely ill, she prayed that God would extend her life long enough to complete her translation. God answered her prayer. On the day she finished proofreading the last page, she died.

Q: Pandita Ramabai had limited influence and faced societal apathy about her causes. How might we succumb to some of the hardships of leadership rather than standing up for God and His commandments?

PORTRAITIST OF COMPASSION

Catherine Gourley, in her book *War, Women, and the News*, tells fascinating stories of female journalists and photojournalists during times of war. Many of them seemed to get behind the scenes and into the hearts of other women struggling with poverty. When unrest began in Europe, female journalists applied for overseas duty alongside soldiers and their male counterparts. One such woman was Anne O'Hare McCormick, who became the first woman to win journalism's highest award—the Pulitzer Prize. Born in England in 1882, her family settled in Columbus, Ohio, where she and her mother struggled financially. Anne's mother sold a book of poetry she wrote by going door-to-door as a way to supplement the income she earned while working at a dry goods store. Later, both Anne and her mother worked for a weekly newspaper.

Anne married when she was 30 and traveled with her husband for his work, which took the couple to Europe. On those travels she kept a journal of the people she met and interviewed. Upon returning, she contacted the editor of *The New York Times* and asked if she could send him some of her stories. The newspaper published them in a column entitled "Abroad." Her writings about dictators, political unrest, and ordinary people led to her receiving the coveted Pulitzer Prize. At her death in 1954, the newspaper edged her final column in black. Just a few months before, she had written about the power of women, who, she said, had a responsibility to help retain the strength of America's moral and spiritual values. "Women, and particularly American women in a time when the United States is thrust into a position of unique power and influence, have the soul of the nation in their keeping."

Q: An obvious leader in a troubling time, McCormick's words still resonate today. Are we, as female leaders in the twenty-first century, the kind of leaders (and women) who take her words seriously and stand to meet the challenge because we "have the soul of the nation" in our keeping?

YOUNG AND LEARNING

Korinne and I met when we served on a church missions committee together. She asked me to mentor her as a leader, and we met regularly to discuss leadership issues she faced. Our meetings weren't face-to-face, however. What worked best for us was to email back and forth on a specific day of the week. Over the months, as I got to know Korinne, I discovered she was a compassionate young woman searching for her ministry niche. A mother of three little guys, she was a stay-at-home mom who wanted to impact her world with the good news of Jesus. We talked about her missions vision and how she saw herself participating in overseas missions. She made a trip to India to investigate the possibility of our church establishing a missions partnership.

When she returned from that trip, however, Korinne decided her place for ministry was in local missions efforts. She coordinated a year-long project in an underserved neighborhood through directing a school backpack program for children, a VBS in the neighborhood park, and a fall pumpkin-carving event for residents. These projects fine-tuned her fledgling leadership skills, and Korinne developed a passion for local missions. She attended an orientation in a nearby metropolitan area and from there became involved in several ministries to international residents. She and her young family also took part in work with Muslims. It wasn't long before Korinne was a "clearing house" of information about local missions opportunities. As she reached out to minister in her neighborhood, she discovered she had to step out of her comfortable lifestyle to reach others with Jesus' love. Not all of Korinne's efforts were successful; not everything went smoothly. But she learned valuable lessons. That's part of leadership, isn't it? Her story isn't finished! She has many years to use her calm approach to leading and her willing spirit to serve.

Q: Do we move through our days focused on the glamorous of the unknown? Or are our hearts touched by the needs of people in our immediate sphere of influence? Do we challenge others to become better leaders and answer God's call on their lives? Our stories aren't finished either!

INVOLVED AND MOTIVATED

I met Tanya when I visited her church to make a missions presentation. Tanya was a single, confident professional interested in anything relating to missions. Her large church gave her many opportunities to take part in a wide variety of activities. Tanya worked with boys at a group home, and her easygoing manner balanced her firm determination to provide guidance for the young men in her care. We got to know one another better when we went on a missions trip to Croatia. Our team was variety personified, and when we arrived, we discovered our diverse team was exactly what the Croatian women had wanted but hadn't specified!

Isn't that how God often works? We represented all ages—a retired woman, a young mother, two middle-aged women, and our single woman, Tanya. And our diversity didn't stop there. Tanya is African-American, our team leader Hispanic, and the three remaining women were from southern and western states. Tanya and I roomed together, and we had such fun as we learned how to brush our teeth without swallowing any tap water!

I wish you could hear Tanya tell the story about the photographer who followed her all over Zagreb, the capital of Croatia, trying to take her picture! We guessed he'd hadn't seen very many African-Americans, and Tanya is very photogenic!

I watched Tanya accept changes in our schedule with gracious flexibility. Her friendly personality touched the Croatian women. As we led workshops and talked with women who had lived through the civil war in the 1990s, Tanya expressed sympathy that came from personal experience. Tanya was familiar with difficult situations. At home she cared for her brother until he passed away in 2013. She experienced grief and heavy responsibility but rose above her difficult circumstances and remained faithful to her obligations.

Several years have passed since our missions trip, and we now live thousands of miles apart, but we've remained connected. Her busy life includes ministry activities, cruises, and family reunions.

Q: Do you let the everyday demands of life interfere when you know you've been called to a specific leadership role? Tanya is an example of a woman who has continued to lead throughout many seasons of her life. Is your attitude a positive one, gentle under pressure?

DETERMINED AND INVESTED

I first met Eva when she gave her testimony at a Women in Evangelism luncheon. She spoke about how she used her home decorating business as an opportunity to share her faith. When I saw her creativity shining through like a strong beacon light, I thought to myself, *Here's a woman I want to get to know! She has great leadership potential.* Years later, Eva and I are firm friends and coleaders, connected by our commitment to excellence. Eva, a pastor's wife, became the coordinator of a Christian Women's Job Corps® site in central California and soon was in demand as a trainer for the ministry program. She moved into leadership with a national missions organization and was soon leading seminars and speaking all over the United States. Did she possess those golden keys of privilege and position? Not at all!

The experiences Eva had in her childhood could have made her a bitter woman. But she chose instead to use her experiences for God's glory by ministering to women affected by poverty, abuse, or unemployment. She felt especially called to women who had no hope and saw no future. Through her life and words, Eva displayed how God has a plan for every woman. Her example encouraged many to finish or continue their education—Eva herself returned to college and earned her master's degree while fulfilling heavy ministry responsibilities. She learned to be an effective leader by using her time wisely, establishing stable relationships with others, and committing to nothing less than excellence in all she did.

Eva now serves in a church denominational position and continues to demonstrate well-defined leadership qualities as she plans women's events and provides leadership training. Eva has not forgotten her beginnings, her Hispanic ethnicity, or her early experiences as a pastor's wife. Her commitment has never wavered even though she has faced difficult circumstances. The old-fashioned word *stalwart* is a good one to describe Eva's approach to leadership. Through her husband's recent cancer diagnosis, she has been resolute. Her own health issues haven't caused her to step away from her vigorous support of missions and ministry. Her childhood may have been less than perfect, but those experiences never undermined her love for others or dimmed her love of life.

Unfaltering in her belief that God wants every family to honor Him and live by His standards, Eva continued to be committed to helping women move out of poverty and into Christ's love. Eva is daring, yes, even audacious. Determined? Eva personifies the word! If one door is closed to women and their needs, she finds another door. She has traveled to New Mexico, Hawaii, Arizona, Texas, and New England to lead training seminars. She has spent weeks overseas training new leaders in Moldova and Croatia. If you were to sit down with Eva, you would quickly discover her passion to help women. She works to lead others to a saving knowledge of Jesus while sharing her life testimony.

Q: How would someone describe your actions or plans? Would they use words like determined *or* invested? *How does your childhood affect your ability to lead? Do you let your past undermine what you do as a leader? Have you moved with God's power beyond your life experiences to achieve what God has called you to do? Or are you stuck in the past with the "what ifs" and "if onlys"?*

FAITHFUL IN CHANGING TIMES

Many of the people I meet or read about connect in unusual ways. I have discovered common interests and backgrounds. That happened when I found a book by Camille Hornbeck about a missionary to India. It was an unexpected link to the story I read years ago about Pandita Ramabai and my new friend's interest in India.

Camille Hornbeck's book, *Rebekah Ann Naylor, M.D.: Missionary Surgeon in Changing Times*, is a comprehensive biography of a remarkable surgeon who answered God's call to India, and it gives readers many insights into Dr. Naylor's life and personality.

The daughter of a former president of Southwestern Baptist Theological Seminary, Rebekah felt impressed in junior high that she should be a doctor. Within a few years, she felt God's calling to medical missions. After graduating with honors from Baylor University in 1964, she attended Vanderbilt University School of Medicine.

Rebekah arrived in India in 1974 to work at the Bangalore Baptist Hospital, where she had surgical duties in addition to overseeing the enlargement of the hospital facilities and broadening the spiritual growth of the institution staff. In 1996, she established the Rebekah Ann Naylor School of Nursing. In addition to her medical duties, she led Bible studies and chapel, and she served as a consultant to the Foreign Mission Board (now International Mission Board) of the Southern Baptist Convention.

Rebekah embraced Indian culture, learned the local language, and according to one source, was the only American he knew who could confidently drive in Indian traffic! Even though she was shy and retiring by nature, she was fervent in her faith, and her standards of excellence permeated all she did. Her love of music led to many hospital and local musical events. Entertaining and travel have been an enormous part of her life. She was an avid letter-writer, corroborated by the more than 4,000 letters she wrote to her parents alone.

Within four years of serving at Bangalore Baptist Hospital, Rebekah became chief of the medical staff and later served as the medical superintendent. Once, the Indian government denied her license to practice medicine, and at times denied or delayed her residential visas, but Rebekah remained true to God's call on her life.

Rebekah retired from the International Mission Board in 2009 and continues to travel to Bangalore twice a year to help with spiritual ministry, administrative issues, and teaching.

Hornbeck, in her biography, said this about Dr. Rebekah Naylor, "A woman of contrasts? Maybe. A woman of contradictions? *Hmmm.* A complex woman? Definitely. A real woman? Decidedly. She laughs. She cries. She has fears. She has courage. In some respects personal changes have occurred; certainly the world and her situations have changed. Her commitment has not changed. She remains Miss Naylor, a multi-layered woman of passions and strong character."

Q: How do we react when disappointments roll over us like a tsunami? Do we remain faithful to God's call to live and lead for Him, or do we just surrender? Are we strong in our faith, realizing that His plan should take precedence over our own desires? Like Naylor, can we move beyond a title and dream and serve God in spite of difficulties?

PROFESSIONAL AND CONFIDENT

Julie is one of six daughters. Under their mother's guidance, she and two of her sisters chose demanding, varying careers. Julie's oldest sister earned three master's degrees and served as the national director of the American Baptist Association. Another sister earned her doctorate in public health and founded Kalusugan, an organization to help fellow Filipinos learn about healthy nutrition.

My friend Julie entered the medical field and started her own home healthcare business. Her business necessitated she navigate the deep waters of state medical board requirements governing home healthcare. Inspections, personnel issues, and quality control dictated long hours and miles of frustration. Julie was the consummate professional as she met with board inspectors and worked with medical professionals who provided quality assistance in homes of recovering patients or those needing long-term care for various reasons.

I visited her busy offices one day in order to take her to lunch. During our time together I asked her to take a leadership position in our organization. Soon Julie began serving as president of a state chapter of a national Christian nursing organization. Her organizational skills were obvious as she led the fledgling group to participate in national activities. On a state level, she helped provide continuing education credits for nurses who attended annual women's events. Anyone could attend the classes, and the instructors gave wonderful, up-to-date information on elder care, diabetes, and nutrition.

As a result of the success of the state chapter, Julie was elected national president, bringing her organizational and professional skills to the position. She gave her new role no less than the 100 percent she gave to everything she tackled.

Still, God was moving in her life, and within several years, Julie sold her home healthcare business and began working on a PhD to help others begin home healthcare businesses. In the past several years she has broadened her healthcare experiences to include hospice and palliative care. She now works in administration as an RN quality coordinator, which includes auditing medical records and educating nurses and therapists about properly documenting records.

Julie's continued education and varied experiences have placed her in a position to provide expertise in three professional areas. Her confidence in providing excellent care and her high standards give evidence of her thirst for knowledge and determination to excel in all she undertakes.

Q: Regardless of our leadership positions, we must strive to be professional. Our preparation and training will make us confident in the work we are given. How have you prepared yourself to lead? Do you exhibit professionalism in every situation you face?

These stories are mere glimpses into these women's complicated lives, but hopefully you've gained insights into what has made them successful and noteworthy as leaders. Do any of the questions challenge your leadership life? Can you make changes that will help you become more effective?

As you read the following chapters, highlight areas where you are struggling to keep your leadership edge. Maybe you should start a list of topics you need to study or items that need your attention. Remember, the purpose of this book is not to simply raise questions about how you lead but to assist you in fine-tuning your leadership skills to enable you to be a risk-taker, courageous, determined, invested, a learner, confident, faithful, and a compassionate woman who takes her leadership responsibilities seriously and approaches them with passion!

CHAPTER 2

What does the Bible say about leadership?

Where do you turn when your child or grandchild asks you a question about right and wrong? What resources do you use when making family decisions or facing a difficult situation at work? Who is your role model for relationships in your life?

As parents, professionals, and social beings, we all develop a network of personal advice-givers for navigating day-to-day living. I have a friend who calls this network her go-to people. As helpful as these individuals try to be, we have all been on the receiving end of poor advice or incomplete information that led us astray or, at the very least, confused us.

Several years ago I worked for the local library. I loved the cozy atmosphere of our small branch and enjoyed introducing customers to the exciting world of reading and discovering information. Seeing the spark in a child's eyes as he or she embarked on a reading adventure was the highlight of my day! Our small staff was directed by a Christian woman, and one day she suggested that we gather once a week to pray for our branch and each other. I was close to a co-worker my age, and one morning as we were getting ready to open, she asked me a question. "When you tell me what you do with women and about things going on in your church, you always seem so sure of your decisions. How do you make your decisions? How can you be certain that what you decide is right? What guides you?"

I tried to explain that while I don't always do what I know is right, my guiding resource is not something that comes from within me. I told her that my yardstick—my guide—is the Bible. It contains what I need to know to make decisions that are pleasing to God. I acknowledged I was often inept in my follow-through but that God's Word provided the answers for right and wrong situations, guidance for my personal relationships, and principles for decision-making.

Reflecting on where God has directed me in leadership positions led me to think about the many times I sought guidance and instruction from the Bible. The Bible is not silent on how leaders are to lead—it covers our attitude, behavior, relationships with others, and many other applicable topics. Examples of successful leaders are plentiful and continue to serve as influential role models.

While many passages in the Bible could be cited as good tutorials for leaders, I have found two that are especially valuable. As we assume various leadership roles, Ecclesiastes 3:1–8 and selections from Proverbs can help us remain focused, grounded in God's Word, and centered on His principles. Let's look at what Scripture has to say before moving on to the questions women leaders have asked about leadership.

> *There is a time for everything,*
>> *and a season for every activity under the heavens:*
> *a time to be born and a time to die,*
>> *a time to plant and a time to uproot,*
> *a time to kill and a time to heal,*
>> *a time to tear down and a time to build,*
> *a time to weep and a time to laugh,*
>> *a time to mourn and a time to dance,*
> *a time to scatter stones and a time to gather them,*
>> *a time to embrace and a time to refrain from embracing,*
> *a time to search and a time to give up,*
>> *a time to keep and a time to throw away,*
> *a time to tear and a time to mend,*
>> *a time to be silent and a time to speak,*

a time to love and a time to hate,
  a time for war and a time for peace.

—ECCLESIASTES 3:1–8

I have always enjoyed reading Ecclesiastes 3. Its verses give us hope in understanding the cycles of life. As we live, we realize everything changes, nothing remains the same. For example, I have been married for more than 40 years. I loved my husband when I married him all those years ago, but the love I have for him now is not the same! Now, be honest... wives don't love *everything* about their husbands. We embrace our husbands' quirks and borderline obsessions as part of their personalities, but there may not be love involved in those things except in the sense of loving the whole "package"!

The writer of Ecclesiastes hammers home the undeniable fact that everything changes. As our lives move from year to year, situation to situation, relationship to relationship, and season to season, we realize that the author of Ecclesiastes was absolutely right. Even if we believe there is no movement, there is! Part of the mystery of this passage of Scripture is that it's difficult to comprehend how to know when to move from season to season. Growing older can't be changed—we can't do anything to move ourselves along in this area. On the contrary, we invest a lot of time in trying to stave off the "ravages of time." But wrinkles will happen!

Other areas aren't as easy to discern, however. A Bible study teacher of mine once explained that while he had learned how to tell time as a child, he had a difficult time knowing when it was "a time to tear down and a time to build" or "a time to love and a time to hate."

I was reading Ecclesiastes 3 several years ago, and I was struck by an application of the verses that I hadn't thought of before. I was doing some personal brainstorming about equipping women to develop as leaders. Perhaps that is why God opened my eyes that day. I had a new understanding that there were some basic principles I could find in the first eight verses of chapter 1 that might help me as I taught others how to be effective leaders. Since that time, I have applied the same Scriptures to other situations in life.

When I began planning my retirement from a key leadership position in my denomination, I saw once again that most of the verses in this passage formed a process that could guide my actions as I "cleaned house"—both emotionally and spiritually—in preparation for the Big Change. So, we can assuredly say that the writer of Ecclesiastes gives us a set of guidelines that can help us work through some seasons of our lives.

So, let's look at how these verses can move us forward as we seek to understand what makes a perceptive, efficient leader. These broad principles can apply to women and men alike, but my comments will be directed primarily to women because that is my passion and my major audience. We'll begin with Ecclesiastes 3:2:

A time to be born and a time to die.

For leaders, there is a good time (maybe even a perfect time, from God's viewpoint), as in every area of life, for a leader to emerge. I'm not referring to when the individual is physically born but rather to the place in her life when she understands the abilities and skills she has learned make her a prime candidate for a specific position. This could be a promotion at work or a natural progression in a volunteer organization. The majority of us are smart enough to recognize that opportune moment when we can step forward and put into practice what we have developed. "A time to be born" can mean all of this for women as we seek to excel and accomplish what we have been equipped to do.

The second part of this verse is a little more problematic. "A time to die" isn't a phrase any of us want to apply to ourselves. Someone else, maybe, but not us! I don't think it necessarily refers to a physical death. As I prepared for retirement or as you look toward moving to another area of your career or community position, there will be a time when you feel things waning. *Waning* is a word we usually apply to the moon, but in this instance I believe it can apply to the leadership process. One definition of *waning* is "fading," and this is how I regard our time as leaders. There will be a specific end to your time of leadership in any given area.

That end could occur, of course, because of your death, but more likely it will be because you feel directed into another area of service as a volunteer or a move within your profession. This is a time of endings. Your associations with co-workers may diminish, your influence may decrease, and your authority may end.

"A time to be born" necessitates we be alert and willing. "A time to die" as leaders dictates that we realize there is an end to every leadership phase and that we should be prepared to make the changes necessary to move on. Learn to tell time!

A time to kill and a time to heal.

How in the world could the first part of Ecclesiastes 3:3 apply to leadership, you ask? When a promotion or retirement is imminent in a leader's life, there will be definite times when she will need to metaphorically kill thoughts and behavior to protect status or set boundaries. There will be a time when our thoughts about what the right thing to do will have to take a backseat because someone else has taken on the responsibilities we once held. Killing thoughts of jealousy (*How could she do that to what I worked so hard to accomplish?*) must happen. Leaving a position—no matter the reason—is often difficult, and there is a tendency to protect our interests. But wait . . . they aren't our interests any longer, are they?

Leaving a leadership role may also necessitate a time of healing. We may need to build or repair bridges. A good leader should continually assess her relationships, but we all know that issues often get swept under the rug of busyness, and unresolved conflicts can fester. No one wants to leave a leadership position under a cloud, so an effective leader will attend to hard feelings and misunderstandings in order to foster healing. It may be time to kill and heal.

A time to tear down and a time to build.

Just as home remodelers tear down walls to create new spaces in their houses, a good leader recognizes the need to dismantle distrust, resentment, competition, and incompetence in order to build a strong organization, a more efficient staff, or weed out unhealthy competition. The tearing down must come from a well-developed plan. It could mean setting aside old methodology and embracing more up-to-date techniques. Leaders must ask themselves if the organization is operating in the past. We know (or should know) what our personal assets are and should have a working knowledge of the competencies of those who perform with, for, or under us.

It is a leader's responsibility to ensure that those on her team and in the organization have a clear understanding of purpose. As she builds strong relationships and establishes new guidelines, she needs to prepare for the coming transitions. Discerning the time to tear down and to build is a critical element for a successful leader. Knowing when to tear down resistance, negativity, or incompetence and how to build up others or a group's ability to move forward is part of telling time.

> *A time to weep and a time to laugh, a time to mourn and a*
> *time to dance.*

If a leader doesn't have a storehouse of memories of humorous incidents and joyous celebrations, she hasn't enjoyed very much of her leadership journey. Every leader should be able to recall comical situations that dissolved everyone in laughter. Reflecting on difficult, sad times should call to mind the lessons you've learned or the experiences that had the proverbial silver linings revealed at a later time. While all of us face leadership incidents that bring tears to our eyes, there should be rays of bright light that shine through, causing us to laugh and dance. When transitions such as promotions, downsizing, retirement, or new directions come, it is not unreasonable to realize, and accept, that everything will not always go smoothly. There *will* be weeping and mourning, but there will also be laughing and dancing! May the weeping and mourning pass quickly; let's get to the laughing and dancing!

> *A time to scatter stones and a time to gather them, a time to*
> *embrace and a time to refrain from embracing.*

No, this isn't a verse about throwing rocks! Although leaders may feel as if others are pelting them with stones, I don't believe this verse is talking about that aspect of leading. I believe this phrase could be applied to the "how" of leadership. By that I mean there are times in my leadership role I have cast my net of influence out and drawn others of like mind in. I have intentionally expanded a team to further the purpose of the broader organization. I have worked intentionally to enlist new leaders and volunteers.

When stones are gathered to build a wall or house, something positive happens. I have scattered stones as I have tried to motivate women to become involved, to contribute, to participate—I observe, create relationships, and provide resources to encourage women to become involved in ministry. Then, as with any effort, the time comes when I have gathered in those "caught in the net."

As in all things related to leadership, timing is critical. Knowing when to scatter and when to gather stones comes from experience, intuition, and preparation. Scattering and gathering is important, but embracing and restraining is just as necessary for the leader. As I thought about the implications for women in leadership, I began to realize that there are times when we need to know what *not* to do. There are some ideas that sound good, but they really aren't! My husband is fond of saying, "Now, there's an idea; not a good idea, but an idea!"

If you have been in any leadership role at work, in your community, at your child's school, or at church, you know that leaders cannot do all that is proposed to them. While it may be a good idea, it might not be for your group or team. It can be worthy, but it's for someone else to tackle. A leader needs to be knowledgeable enough to pick and choose based on sound advice, research, and insight. Some things simply aren't feasible even though the proposal sounds wonderful. For example, our women's ministries team was asked to provide all the meals for funerals at our church. This was requested because that's the way it had been done in the past. Our team at that time only had one member who didn't work outside the home, and, in a church of more than 2,500 members, can you imagine how time-consuming that project would be? A good idea? Of course. Something that needed to be done? Yes. A good match for our team's abilities? Not at all.

So, recognize that you and your team cannot be everything to everyone. Challenges grow you as a leader, but not everything falls within your ability, interest, or within the confines of feasibility. Again, timing is everything.

A time to search and a time to give up, a time to keep and a time to throw away.

We've all lost things—an article of clothing, eyeglasses, or car keys. I remember an incident my husband and I still laugh about that happened when our oldest son was about three years old. We had plans to visit my in-laws for a family get-together and were all ready to leave when we discovered the car keys were nowhere to be found. We scoured the house, looked in the car, and checked coat and pants pockets, all to no avail. The keys were simply gone. In desperation my husband told our son who had been watching our frantic search, "Wayne, if you can find the keys, I'll give you ten cents." Wayne calmly walked over to the fireplace hearth, reached into a decorative old pewter vase and lifted its lid. He reached inside, pulled out the missing keys, and said, "Ta-da!" Then, of course, he held out his hand for his dime!

Just as we waste minutes and even hours looking for missing items, we spend precious time searching for things as leaders. I have invested huge amounts of time searching for trainable women to provide fresh leadership for organizations. Often my search resulted in capable, equipped leaders who accepted leadership roles and helped move us toward our goals. Other times, however, I had to admit that my search produced no results; it was "time to give up." It simply wasn't the right time to search.

Knowing when to keep looking and when to stop the search is a leadership skill that is learned. Experience and insight fuel these successes. Sometimes the search just doesn't yield any results. At this point we should be asking God to direct or redirect our search. It could be we are looking in the wrong place. We might be rushing ahead of Him! Giving up isn't in our nature, so we can be slow to admit that our time is not being spent well. I had a supervisor once tell me, "Place your efforts where you'll get the most bang for your buck." He wasn't speaking only in a financial sense but about being able to see which efforts were producing results.

When I reread the second part of Ecclesiastes 3:6, I couldn't help but remember what I experienced when I retired from a leadership position I'd held for 15 years. I set a retirement date, and in my mind I began the "keep and throw away" journey. Because of the nature of my work, I had accumulated masses of paper items—brochures, maps, speeches, handouts, organizational leaflets, and the list goes on! It took weeks to go through everything and make decisions about what to keep and what needed to be tossed.

Just yesterday I discovered a box of memorabilia from a centennial celebration. Who will want the items when I am gone? The answer comes quickly, "No one!" My home office was another collection of things that needed to be reduced. Which items would be helpful to the person who came after me? Which meant something only to me? Bags, boxes, and piles of stuff later, I came to the realization that keeping and throwing away wasn't a job for wimps!

I really don't think the author of Ecclesiastes was thinking about weeding out paperwork or dated materials when he penned this passage. I do believe, however, that an effective leader should be able to differentiate between what is necessary for her work and what needs to be discarded. Maybe you'll find yourself in a new position where you've inherited processes, traditions, and loads of "stuff." A new leader needs to move slowly as she develops a sense of what needs to be kept and what should go. The wisdom to make these choices can potentially determine how successful a leader will be in her new role.

When I was hired to coordinate a large women's volunteer organization, I asked my father, a long-time pastor, for his advice about approaching my new responsibilities. I have never forgotten his response. He said, "Listen carefully, and don't make any changes for the first six months."

What great advice! Even though you may already know what needs to be changed, what works, and what doesn't work, be sensitive to others' investments in the enterprise and move slowly and cautiously. I'm not saying you should be tentative and nervous. I am saying that even if it's obvious there are undercurrents and challenges, a wise leader will look for sound counsel and establish her credibility before making far-reaching decisions.

Search, give up, keep, and throw away—these are indeed words of a man who exhibited great wisdom in his interactions with others.

> *A time to tear and a time to mend, a time to be silent and a*
> *time to speak.*

If you want to be a credible, effective leader, you must learn about timing! A comedian's success depends on his or her ability to intuit the right time and way to deliver a joke's punch line. Have you ever heard someone trying to tell a joke, and instead it fell flat? That's because the timing was off.

If we want to be leaders who understand the importance of timing, we have to work at learning when to dismantle processes, deconstruct organizations, and even demolish something outdated that might hurt our purpose. I believe this is an interpretation of the phrase in verse 7, "a time to tear and a time to mend." None of us want to be remembered as "that person who took everything apart and then left!" Our tearing needs to be done cautiously and with sensitivity for what is best.

I was a member of a midsize church several years ago that faced changes—that tearing down part. I was taking a graduate course on implementing change at the time, and one of my textbooks stressed the importance of preparing people for coming change. Our pastor gathered a team that had the same vision as he for remodeling our sanctuary. Now, you know this type of change can be fraught with tension and conflict. He laid out the reasoning behind the changes and moved forward in phases, drawing others into the process. Over a period of six months, they guided our thinking, and soon we embraced the idea because we came to understand the value of the proposed changes.

Not only does the "tearing" need to be carefully planned and executed, the mending must be swift and thorough. When we assume the role of change agents, we will almost certainly need to mend bridges, rebuild relationships, and reset fence posts along the way! Part of being an effective leader is paying attention to those who have gone before and now offer a wealth of information.

There is probably nothing more important in the life of a leader than knowing when to be silent and when to speak. Reread that statement! Even though you may be right and your comments insightful, there are times when you need to stay quiet. The inclination to speak your mind can be the death knell of your credibility and influence. People will forgive a lot of things, but speaking in haste isn't one of them. You may know things others don't know, but resisting the urge to put it all out there may be the smartest thing you'll ever do.

Most leaders occasionally find themselves in the position of having the information iceberg—that is, you have a fuller picture, more experience, or access to more facts. Just because we possess all this information doesn't mean it is the best time to reveal our knowledge. A skilled leader is sensitive to timing issues and knows how critical it is to speak when she should and keep silent when necessary.

I believe one particular issue needs to be addressed at this point—confidentiality. Leaders have conversations, read memos, and attend meetings where confidential material is presented and discussed. A good leader is careful not to reveal information that could undermine authority, damage reputations, or cause conflict. This also calls for discernment, as confidentiality doesn't absolve a leader from taking a stand or being an advocate for a cause. When our convictions are challenged or our knowledge can help minimize hurt feelings, misunderstandings, or ruined careers, we must take action to help disarm a volatile situation. With God's guidance, our intervention can bring positive resolution instead.

A time to love and a time to hate, a time for war and a time for peace.

At first, this verse may be difficult to apply to any of your leadership roles, but I believe if you stop and think about the two phrases a bit, you'll see these words can relate directly to verse 6. When we find ourselves in less-than-desirable situations, ones that require courage and commitment, we may try to pass the hard decisions on to someone else. Have you ever said, "They don't pay me enough to do this," or, "Let the boss follow through on this"? As women leaders, we may minimize our abilities and try to take a smaller role than our position warrants. When it's obvious an action or decision must be made, we need to be courageous enough to rise to the challenge and move forward.

Our actions may not be popular. When is any leader's decisions accepted by everyone? Stepping out under God's leadership may force us into a difficult position as advocates for what is right in His eyes. Our verbal support on an issue at work or in our community may put us in the limelight. While we may enjoy the limelight at times, we usually don't want to be there because of others' negatives opinions. If you are a new leader or have new responsibilities, there will be a time when you must decide whether you will be part of the problem or an avenue to a solution. When you "hate" incompetence and speak up about it, you won't be the most popular person at work.

Many years ago my husband and I were active in a volunteer organization and held several leadership roles. Over a period of time we began to see evidence that things were not as they should be in upper management. Others complained to us. We finally had to tell them that they needed to express their grievances directly to management. We spoke for ourselves but would not let them abdicate their responsibility to do the same. They didn't want to take a stand even though all of us thought the same way. The result? Even though they knew we agreed with them, their convictions dissolved, and at the largest fundraiser event of the year, none of the complainers would sit with us at our table! Leadership comes with a price, and part of the price we pay is to realize that it takes courage, commitment, and true concern as we decide when it is time to make war, keep the peace, and love or hate what is wrong.

I recently found a website that specialized in novelty watches. As I scrolled through the pages, I found hundreds of watches featuring birds, animals, skulls, butterflies, graphic designs, and all kinds of cutesy sayings. One watch face was black, and its white lettering simply said, "What time is it?" Read the words of Solomon again. It's true that they point to a discernment of seasons and phases of our lives. However, his words also offer words of wisdom for us as leaders. What time is it? It's time to do some things that at first glance seem negative, but a closer look reveals they can be positive.

As we grow as leaders and plant, demolish, cry, scatter, embrace, search, and keep, we will become sensitive to others' needs. We'll understand how to lead more effectively. It's easy to make a list of negatives, isn't it? If we aren't careful, we can turn Solomon's comments into a list of dos and don'ts. I don't believe that was his intent. From this brief study, I'm suggesting that even though some of these actions seem negative, an effective leader will have to engage in doing all of these things at the right time. Our obligation is to seek God's direction in every decision we make as leaders. The harvesting, healing, building, laughing, dancing, embracing, gathering, giving up, giving away, and speaking will take on new meaning when we prepare to lead at work, in our homes and communities, and in other areas of our lives.

Years ago while leading a statewide women's organization, our leadership team stressed women's need to grow as leaders. I ordered pens with these words: "Equipping women with key skills and godly attitudes for maximum influence." Isn't that how we need to spend our time—equipping women?

Now, let's spend some time investigating what the Book of Proverbs says about leadership.

BIBLICAL BASIS FOR LEADERSHIP FROM PROVERBS

No matter your leadership role, the principles are the same. You may work as a volunteer coordinator of a community food pantry or as a member on a missions trip. You might have signed a contract to commit to a short-term research project for a medical facility. Perhaps you have been asked to serve as the enlistment leader for your church's various ministries. You may be coordinating engaging community sites for the ministry program. The instructions in Proverbs are not for "key" leaders only. Any leader worth her salt is a key leader! Regardless of your leadership role, the influence you have on others cannot be minimized.

Many times we have the mistaken notion that if our name doesn't appear on a corporate letterhead, the way we perform our leadership roles doesn't matter. We may think our efforts are looked at (by ourselves or others) as somehow less important than the seemingly more official ones. That simply isn't true, and I believe the passage from Ecclesiastes cited above proves that to us. Even a casual reading shows that God cares about how we lead.

Let's look at what Proverbs has to say about leaders. I've divided the verses into several categories to facilitate a discussion of desired characteristics, leader responsibilities, and behavior.

A LEADER'S LIFE

Our entire lives as leaders must be examples of godly behavior. Just because we have a title and its accompanying responsibilities, we have no right to conduct our duties any way we choose. We are to keep our emotions under control as Proverbs 16:14–15 (*The Message*) says: "An intemperate leader wreaks havoc in lives; you're smart to stay clear of someone like that. Good-tempered leaders invigorate lives; they're like spring rain and sunshine." We are to be known for our integrity: "So— join the company of good men and women, keep your feet on the tried-and-true paths" (2:20 *The Message*). We are to treat our followers with respect as we motivate them rather than manipulate them: "A good leader motivates, doesn't mislead, doesn't exploit" (16:10 *The Message*). Our dealings with others should reflect our submission to God: "Good leadership is a channel of water controlled by God; he directs it to whatever ends he chooses" (21:1 *The Message*).

A LEADER'S VISION

As we handle the tasks we've been given, we must stay focused on the goals we've set. Wise leaders consult others in their planning: "Refuse good advice and watch your plans fail; take good counsel and watch them succeed" (15:22 *The Message*). Always strive for excellence: "Leaders who know their business and care keep a sharp eye out for the shoddy and cheap" (20:8 *The Message*). An effective leader is always learning: "Like the horizons for breadth and the ocean for depth, the understanding of a good leader is broad and deep" (25:3 *The Message*). She uses her influence in a positive way, as stated in Proverbs 14:28 (*The Message*): "The mark of a good leader is loyal followers; leadership is nothing without a following."

A LEADER'S BEHAVIOR

Even though we may think what we are doing in our small part of the world doesn't matter much, our behavior speaks volumes about our commitment and compassion to carry out God's call on our lives. Our behavior is noticed—always. We must balance love and truth (20:28 *The Message*) and understand that our attitudes, speech, and reactions will be noticed, and we will probably hear about them in the future! As we deal with problems and wrongdoing (16:12), we need to remember our sphere of influence is only as strong as our actions are God-centered. Proverbs 28:2 (*The Message*) tells us that understanding from God will help us meet leadership challenges: "When the country is in chaos, everybody has a plan to fix it—But it takes a leader of real understanding to straighten things out."

Proverbs is a great book to study for its practical applications to many aspects of daily life. The writers of Proverbs don't mince words and definitely call leaders to accountability. We have *not* arrived. We *don't* have all the answers. We are *not* exempt from doing what we know to be right.

Women who want to excel in leadership—those who desire to influence others for God's glory—must rise above the temptation to use their position to unfairly sway others' opinions and actions. Rather, effective leaders must strive to incorporate the teachings of this great Book of Proverbs:

> *Their purpose is to teach people wisdom and discipline, to help them understand the insights of the wise. Their purpose is to teach people to live disciplined and successful lives, to help them do what is right, just, and fair. These proverbs will give insight to the simple, knowledge and discernment to the young. Let the wise listen to these proverbs and become even wiser. Let those with understanding receive guidance by exploring the meaning in these proverbs and parables, the words of the wise and their riddles. Fear of the LORD is the foundation of true knowledge, but fools despise wisdom and discipline.*
>
> —PROVERBS 1:2–7 NLT

DISCUSSION QUESTIONS TO USE FOR A STUDY OF LEADERSHIP PRINCIPLES IN PROVERBS

1. What might happen if a leader does not follow the principles found in Proverbs? Give an example of what happens when leaders do not conduct their lives by God's standards.

2. What part do a leader's emotions play in her leadership roles?

3. Why is it important for a leader to have a vision? What happens when there is no vision?

4. Why should a leader always be a learner?

5. How will a balance of love and truth in a leader's behavior impact the influence she has?

6. Make a list of attributes a leader should personify as she strives to focus on being God-centered.

WHAT'S NEXT?

Now that you have learned about the timeliness involved in leading and some practical suggestions from Proverbs about our lives, vision, and behavior, turn to the table of contents, and look at the questions the women I surveyed asked about leadership. I believe some of your questions will be the same. You may choose to read the chapters that answer your specific questions, or you might decide to read straight through and take the questions as they come, gleaning insights as you go.

No one can completely understand the frustrations, challenges, or specific needs you may have because they are unique to your leadership roles and circumstances. However, some leader somewhere (whom you may never meet) may have experienced something similar enough to your situation to give you some words of wisdom.

This is the purpose of this collection on how we as women lead, how we balance various aspects of our lives as we lead, and how God wants to work through us (not in spite of us!) for His glory.

Read on!

CHAPTER 3

♦

What helps you maintain balance in your life and establish boundaries?

While attending a women's evangelism luncheon, I had an interesting conversation with the young woman coordinating the event. We discussed how we were both struggling to balance all our leadership responsibilities so they didn't consume every moment of our lives. She told me about a mentoring situation she'd had when she first became a believer. An elderly man offered to mentor her as she studied the Bible and searched for God's plan for her life.

When they were talking one day about time management, her wise mentor said it was important to know which of the balls you were juggling were fragile glass ones and which ones could survive being dropped. The glass balls of our lives are those most precious and meaningful to us: our relationship to Christ, our marriage, our family, our health, and our friends. The other balls such as work, community projects, church life, and recreational activities can survive an occasional drop. He further shared that when we juggle too many responsibilities and take on too many obligations, we are flirting with the likelihood of failure in some of those areas. The result of imbalance is a loss of vision and perspective and the inability to discern what is most important.

This analogy has helped me become more cautious in accepting new responsibilities. What I am doing may be a good thing, but if it causes me to drop one of my glass balls, it isn't for me—at least at that time!

This chapter will focus on three areas that will help leaders keep the most important balls in their lives in the air: balance, boundaries, and burnout.

PRIORITIZING BALANCE

How often are your conversations peppered with words like *coping*, *overcommitted*, *pressured*, *overwhelmed*, and *priorities*? An important factor of being a strong leader is learning how to integrate work into our active personal lives. Your commitments, even though you chose to accept them, add more balls to the ones you're already juggling. And now, thanks to smartphones, none of us are ever free from emails, text messages, or phone calls, which adds a stressful sense of urgency to less important tasks. Pressure to perform at work intrudes even on family vacations, making it almost impossible to focus on relaxing and being with family.

I recently lead conferences for an event attended by 2,000 women. As I waited for one session to begin, I talked with three women attending together. When one woman's phone rang, she left the room to answer, and her friend explained. Her new job demanded she be on call virtually 24/7. The poor woman paid her registration fee and part of the hotel bill only to spend most of the weekend standing in a hallway solving problems and answering questions over the phone! The spiritual renewal she had been seeking became a glass ball that shattered when it hit the ground.

Most of us have had at least one of those aha moments when we realize we have taken on too much and added new commitments and obligations to an already crowded schedule. We know that something has to be done! But how can we achieve balance in our lives? There are five areas of our lives that must be in balance if we are to have any chance of being effective leaders and sane women.

1. SPIRITUAL GROWTH: This is a glass ball that won't bounce! Harold Myra in *The Leadership Secrets of Billy Graham* tells the story of

Graham talking about feeling empty and poorly equipped for ministry. The person he spoke with told Graham he was like a water pump that was pumping from ground water rather than deep well water. He needed to deepen his relationship with Christ, therefore deepening his reserve. Aren't we like this? We neglect Bible study and prayer and expect to draw from reservoirs that are nearly dry. Only by drawing from the Living Water will we be ready for difficulties and challenging leadership situations.

2. PERSONAL LIFE: Order in your personal life may mean something different to me than it does to you. For instance, I won't leave the house if my bed isn't made. I detest coming into my house and seeing a sink full of dirty dishes. When these things are done, I feel a sense of order. I try to make my time count at home, just as I do work. To maintain order, I make lists of things I need to do around the house. Other areas of my life may be crammed full of duties I must perform, and I may feel unproductive there, but at least, I feel better if there's a semblance of order in my personal life.

3. EMOTIONAL HEALTH: Our emotions can create a tornado of imbalance that has others running away from us. If you are known at work as volatile or your nickname at home is "Mom the Bomb," it's time to step back and assess how you react to circumstances. You may need to take your child out of the time-out chair and sit there yourself! My son-in-law uses this technique in running his home improvement business. I once ordered custom-made pantry doors for him to install and waited six long weeks. When they finally arrived, and he went to pick them up at the home improvement store, he discovered one was damaged. Not only was all that waiting for nothing, he wouldn't earn any money that day! Irritated, he stepped away, spent a few moments in "time out," and prayed before handling the damage with the store. Emotions can cause a situation to escalate, and before we know it, things have spiraled out of control. There's no balance in a situation like that!

4. PHYSICAL HEALTH: When I lose sleep, I'm not at my best. My mind whirls away the hours of the night, and I get up out of sorts and stumble through the day. Therefore, I have made it a practice not to work on projects that might keep me thinking long into the dark hours! Instead of stirring creativity, these hours are wasted with tossing and turning. I try to relax and let myself wind down at the end of each day. Healthy eating habits can also help me stay balanced. Healthy eating not only sustains our bodies, but it feeds healthier emotions that enable us to do our best. Take care of yourself, and the results will be daytime hours that are more productive and happier. Find a system that works for you—and maintain your physical condition through exercise, proper sleep, and healthy eating.

5. WORK LIFE: Your work responsibilities must be kept in perspective. The pressure that comes from employers and assigned tasks are often out of our control, so we have to deal with them to the best of our abilities. However . . . when we decide our work is a glass ball instead of a rubber one, this will have a huge impact on all the other balls we're juggling. Long hours, demanding bosses, heavy travel schedules, and difficult co-workers can drain us and leave us scrambling to fit God, spouses, family, and friends into our lives somehow. We must be vigilant regarding our work while keeping those responsibilities balanced with the rest of our lives.

> There's enough time today to do everything God expects.
> If you simply can't get it done, maybe it's not yours to do.
> —PENELOPE STOKES, *WOMEN IN LEADERSHIP*

ACHIEVING BALANCE

There's not much argument against the value of living a balanced life! The problem comes when we try to figure out the "how to" of the issue.

Psalm 139:5 assures us God is ever-protecting in His vigilant care for us, "You hem me in behind and before, and you lay your hand upon me." We must turn to Him for guidance in how we order our days, weeks, months, and years. In her book, *Knit Together: Discover God's Pattern for Your Life*, Debbie Macomber says, "If we are truly intent on following God's purpose for our lives, balance is a key part of the equation, and I believe balance is achievable only when we put God first."

Macomber uses knitting patterns to illustrate the value of following God's patterns to make decisions and work through difficult life situations in order to have healthy relationships. My grandmother taught me how to crochet, but I often struggled to follow the written patterns for baby blankets, vests, and hats. Graney made her own patterns and could work her way through the stitches with a beautiful set of baby booties or an afghan as a result. Me? If I don't have a pattern, I can't make a thing!

Isn't that the way we often approach balancing our lives? We have a pattern outlined in God's Word, but our selfish attitudes make us think we know better. Or we may think we can do things on our own, and the results are less than what God wants for us. Life's situations and leadership challenges fall apart under our misdirection. We are so sure we have everything under control and are confident in our abilities. If we want our lives to reflect God, we must follow His patterns set out in His Word. We become distracted, and before we know it, we have a mess! I was crocheting a baby blanket while watching a television game show. You might guess how that turned out! I discovered a complete round later that I had put three double crochets in a corner instead of six, creating a lopsided corner. Life is like that when we don't follow the perfect pattern. Instead of finding satisfaction in a job well done, we must back up and unravel our mistakes before we can go forward.

Here's what the psalmist said in Psalm 119:4–8 (*The Message*):

> You, GOD, prescribed the right way to live; now you expect us to
> live it. Oh, that my steps might be steady, keeping to the course
> you set; then I'd never have any regrets in comparing my life
> with your counsel. I thank you for speaking straight from your
> heart; I learn the pattern of your righteous ways. I'm going to
> do what you tell me to do; don't ever walk off and leave me.

When your doctor writes a prescription for you, do you take it? Of course you do! What's the point of going to see a doctor if you don't follow his or her instructions? Why then is it that we don't listen to what God tells us to do? Our stubborn spirit overrules His perfect prescriptions for living a balanced and God-directed life. He wants obedience from us—"now you expect us to live it."

Following I've listed some practical suggestions for achieving balance. They are nothing new, but we must incorporate these practices into our lives so they become as natural as breathing. Make them your go-to actions to stay in balance.

✦ *Do Not Procrastinate:* Stay on time or keep ahead of schedule to relieve stress, lower your blood pressure, and give you peace of mind.

✦ *Pray and Seek God's Guidance:* This should be the first thing you do when balance flies out the window. His solutions are always perfect!

✦ *Stay Positive and Expect Good Results:* Do you enjoy your work? If not, how can you change that? Begin by looking for something good in every circumstance. A positive attitude will infiltrate every area of your life, and it won't be long until your family, friends, co-workers, and neighbors notice a difference.

✦ *Relax:* Your daily obligations can be demanding, and if you don't learn to pray for calmness, breathe deeply, and exercise, you may never achieve the balance you want.

LAST THOUGHTS ON BALANCE

Achieving balance is not a "once done, always done" exercise. Most of us will struggle with this issue all our lives. I called an insurance agent for an appointment and mentioned that we could meet early in the morning. His immediate response was, "Well, that might not work. I'm in charge of getting my three kids ready for school, and it doesn't take much for things to go completely off course!" Like him, one small incident throws our plan for balance out the window. Family demands, work responsibilities, and other commitments can cause imbalance. Here are questions that relate to the importance of being positive, staying focused, and avoiding overload. Answer them honestly and evaluate where you are in your home life, work life, and relationships with others.

Q: Is my work challenging? Do I have fun at work? Is my job a good fit with my abilities and interests?

Q: Do I have hobbies? What do I do with my family? Is my family supportive of me? Are my relationships with family members healthy?

Q: Do I have friends outside work? How would I rate my social life? How often do I see my friends?

Q: Am I an informed citizen? Do I participate in community activities?

Q: Am I healthy? Do I exercise regularly? How are my eating habits? How much sleep do I get each night? Am I comfortable with my body?

Q: What am I doing to grow spiritually? Do I have a regular quiet time to read the Bible and pray? Does my family have special times together to talk about God?

Q: How would I rate my emotional health? Do I have a healthy self-esteem? How do I challenge myself intellectually?

ESTABLISHING BOUNDARIES

Another commonly asked question in my leadership survey revolved around how to establish healthy boundaries. Boundaries help define our responsibilities, speak to our abilities, and reflect our leadership approach. So, let's look at how well-defined boundaries affect our lives.

When we begin to establish the boundaries of a new job or relationship, we realize boundaries and convictions have a lot in common. Not all boundaries will be popular! But, you knew that already, didn't you? As a newlywed, I established a humorous boundary (but I meant it). I told my husband I married him for better or worse but not for lunch! If he was near the house and came in for lunch, I was unavailable to make sandwiches or clean up the kitchen. We've laughed about it through the years, but he doesn't even ask any more! A silly thing but a boundary nevertheless.

We must be masters at establishing boundaries. In the home we often set procedures in motion about laundry, making beds, cleaning the kitchen, and picking up toys. As our families grow we move on to boundaries about phone calls, curfews, dating, and homework. Establishing boundaries in the home may seem never-ending, even when our children become adults. Then, there are boundaries about college tuition, moving back home, and employment. It isn't long until we set boundaries about what grandchildren can (or can't) do on our sofas!

We know what would happen if we failed to establish boundaries. *Chaos* is the word that comes to my mind. All of us need boundaries; they create filters through

> CONSIDER THE IMPACT OF THESE STATISTICS FROM DAVID COTTRELL'S *LEADERSHIP . . . BIBLICALLY SPEAKING:*
>
> - Only 14 percent of leaders are seen by their followers as someone they would choose as a role model.
> - Less than 50 percent of people trust their leaders.
> - 61 percent of business leaders don't exhibit appropriate managerial behavior.
> - 40 percent of leaders are threatened by talented followers.
> - 40 percent of employees say their leaders do a poor job of solving problems.
> - US corporations lose half of their customers in five years, half of their employees in four years, and half of their investors in less than one year.
> - 50 percent of employees say their leaders tolerate poor performance for too long.
> - What do these statistics reveal? People want—and need—strong, stable leaders!

which we can make sound decisions that create healthy personalities and productive people.

The Bible is not silent on this subject. We will be better equipped to deal with life and leadership situations if we have established some biblical boundaries ahead of time. Look up the following references to see how God intends for us to conform our actions to His plan.

1 John 2:15: Do my boundaries cause me to live differently from the ways of the world?

2 Corinthians 12:10: Do my boundaries prepare me to face persecution?

Luke 12:34: Does how I look at material possessions influence my life boundaries?

Luke 22:42: How do my boundaries reflect how I feel about my personal rights?

Galatians 6:2: Do my boundaries isolate me or am I involved in the lives of others?

Mark 8:38: What is my reaction to Jesus' words?

When leaders get serious about establishing boundaries, there is no resource more valuable than God's Word. However, it isn't always easy to establish boundaries, nor will they always be welcomed and accepted by others, as I already mentioned. Some may regard your boundaries as infringements on their rights (and they may be!) while others may see your boundaries are connected to something they don't agree with. This is where our leadership responsibilities come with a price tag. Leadership demands setting boundaries because they relate to how we carry out our responsibilities. For example, you may set aside Monday afternoons for spiritual growth study, and you refuse to schedule any activity that interferes with it. A new team member who needs training can only meet on Monday afternoons. What about your boundary? In this instance, you might choose to be flexible, fulfill your duties, and move a boundary (at least temporarily).

Proverbs 11:3 says that integrity must guide us in making decisions that are godly. My survey revealed that while women wanted to know their leaders on a personal level, they also had numerous questions about setting boundaries as leaders themselves. They wanted to know the "real" person behind the leadership title, but in establishing their own boundaries, they were interested in how their leaders kept their boundaries intact.

Our effectiveness as leaders will, in part, be determined by how strong we are in maintaining boundaries. Isn't it easier to sometimes set them aside? We want to please everyone, so we adjust the lines we've drawn. When we do that, our followers (and family, friends, and co-workers) see us as vacillating rather than stabilizing. We must remain confident in the boundaries we set and not waiver at the first sign of opposition. If the boundary is important, it stays. If it isn't important, why set it as a boundary? This doesn't discount the flexibility a leader should have but creates a healthy meter in determining what stays and what goes.

ATTITUDE: ANOTHER IMPORTANT WORD RELATED TO BOUNDARIES

Maya Angelou once said, "You can tell a lot about a person by the way he or she handles these three things: a rainy day, lost luggage, and tangled Christmas lights." Don't think, even for a moment, your actions are not noticed. You can whisper your fury into a wastebasket at work and someone may hear! What does a rainy day do to you? Do you delight in the rain God sends or grumble that it interrupts your plans? Can everyone in the vicinity hear your tirade about your missing suitcase? Oh, and those pesky lights! Tangled just to mess with your mood!

When establishing boundaries at work, home, or church, your attitude will carry you further than you think. Others will notice how you say no. Saying no to activities outside your boundaries is hard to do, isn't it?

We often feel as though no one understands why we say no and may be convinced no one cares why we say no. Yet your boundaries will make it easier to use that two-letter word because you have a supporting conviction or statement to back it up.

I read about an Olympian rower who, when asked about the possible bad weather on the day of his event, stated that wind, rain, or losing an oar were all potentialities outside his boat—they are simply out of his control. Our boundaries provide us with guidelines, which means we don't have to make the same type of decision over and over. We can make our decision and move on!

You may be reading this and saying to yourself, "Yeah, right! She doesn't know how hard it is for me to say no!" Saying no can be extremely difficult. Especially if it's for a worthy project. So, here are four reasons that might help you say that little word. First, you can say no when the request has low value for your purpose and goals. Second, you can say no if it's the wrong solution or an answer to the wrong problem. In other words, it's outside your boat! Third, if it's unethical or illegal, it'll be easy to say no. Last, you can say no if the request doesn't meet your professional standards. (This could be true of a decision about a family outing, a church event, or community activity.)

I was once approached by a leader who wanted me to provide child-care for one of his events. Did he want a day camp? No. Could we provide a missions fair? No. What he wanted were women who would babysit. It was easy to say no because it was the wrong venue for us, and it didn't meet the standards and boundaries we had established. It was definitely "outside our boat!"

Someone has referred to attitude as the secret sauce in establishing meaningful boundaries. Isn't that a great term? I love to make gravy to go with pork chops or roast. But my grandkids wouldn't have any of it! I guess they didn't like the sound of the word *gravy* because once I started calling it "sauce," they eagerly took some! A sauce can be bland or spicy. Our attitude is the same: it can simply be or it can overshadow everything on the plate. A little bit of spice goes a long way! A negative attitude can ruin our reputation, undermine a project, and make us unproductive as leaders.

Lost luggage, rainy days, and tangled Christmas lights can be attitude-benders. Leaders need to avoid reacting unfavorably to life's daily irritations. Our boundaries should be of the quality that mold our thoughts and actions and enable us to lead others to reach their potential and goals. When there are negative persons on our teams and in our groups, we should take steps to disarm their negativity. Your boundaries at work should help you do this with success. Mentally block the negativity. Do not let it infiltrate your organization, period! Set a boundary regarding negative behavior, and stick to it. Consider the impact your words have, choose your words carefully, and hold the boundary. In the workplace the boundaries you establish about attitude will determine the atmosphere of your office.

What boundaries do you have about criticizing others? Are there boundaries regarding worrisome issues such as downsizing and unreasonable requests from upper management? If you have not established boundaries about attitude (yours and others') at work, now would be a good time to do so. The following situations may help you think about your attitude boundaries.

❑ **If you are the employee**—Make a list of actions you can take to make your workplace better. Small things can make a difference. Your own attitude counts.

❑ **If you are the employer**—If you are sullen and difficult to get along with, your work environment will mirror that attitude. Everyone's attitude will be better if you are knowledgeable and approachable.

❑ **If your personal attitude isn't positive**—Think about the things you enjoy doing and about the things under your control. Freshen your work space and make it more personal. Consider the silver linings you've found in difficult times and work at being more positive.

We have seen how beneficial achieving balance is for our personal and leadership lives. If we can do these two things, we will be in a strong position to avoid burnout. I was surprised when my surveys revealed burnout wasn't a hot topic. This may be an indication that women are managing their time more, and I am optimistic that achieving balance is easier.

While I'm trying to be optimistic, I'm afraid the survey results do not reflect an increase in balanced lives but instead indicate we have set aside things of value and accepted a diminished quality of life. Have you seen the television commercial about cable connections that depicts a family who has "settled?" They are dressed in colonial costumes and are doing everything the old fashioned way. They are settlers. I don't know about you, but I don't want to settle in life! Rather, I want to live a godly life that is pleasing to my Creator. I want balance in my life and stable boundaries that help me make decisions relating to others.

In Philippians and 2 Timothy, Paul talks about our attitude and general approach to life. His thoughts can help us as we work to avoid burnout in our lives. He says:

✓ Don't focus on your mistakes (Philippians 3:13–14)
✓ Think positively (Philippians 4:13)
✓ Don't be fearful (2 Timothy 1:7)

Even when we have achieved balance and established strong boundaries, we may suffer burnout—that is often the nature of human existence. It doesn't mean we have done anything wrong. It could be a time of testing and a time God will use to teach us a valuable lesson. The key to dealing with burnout is: Deal with it! Assess your situation and determine what changes you can make. Get all the facts because you can't make good decisions if your information is incomplete. Take actions to improve what you can, but be honest about your negative reactions and emotions. It doesn't help to be hard on yourself or blame others. Accepting responsibility is important so you can ask for forgiveness if you need to. Work within the boundaries you've established. Pray about your situation and then . . . let it go!

How many balls are you juggling? Wife, mother, sister? Daughter, caregiver, employee? Boss, volunteer, cook? Counselor, friend, neighbor?

Are you juggling ministry responsibilities, health issues, or homeschooling? Which ones are glass balls? Which ones will shatter if you drop them? Some will bounce; others will never be the same. There isn't enough superglue to mend them. Leaders must spend quality time learning to achieve balance, establishing boundaries, and avoiding burnout. There is no substitute for any of these things. If we fail to live in balance, honor God-directed boundaries, or avoid burnout, we will be ineffective leaders. You may take your children to church, teach a community Bible study group, head a task force at work, or draw your neighborhood together to help a needy family, but having a title doesn't define you as a leader, does it?

In *The DNA of Leadership*, author Judith Glaser says, "The choice about how you lead is yours. You can erect a silo, or construct a campus; you can install a court of law, or an institution of higher learning; you can instill a fear of change and of making mistakes, or the excitement about what is possible; you can build walls, or bridges; you can stifle, or you can resuscitate; you can dictate, or communicate; you can discourage, or you can inspire. It just depends on how you express the vital genes of your leadership DNA."

DO THIS ONE THING

Complete the following sentences:

1. I am known for _____

_____

_____

2. This time next year, I want to be known for _____

_____

_____

3. A current project is challenging me to _____

    _____

    _____

4. I've learned these things in the past three months: _____

    _____

    _____

5. One problem I solved recently: _____

    _____

    _____

6. I have established a new boundary: _____

    _____

    _____

Pay Dirt

The idiom "pay dirt" means, "earth or ore that yields a profit to a miner; a useful or remunerative discovery or object." Each chapter will have a Pay Dirt section summarizing the chapter's message and to point out the profitable discoveries for a leader. Here's the Pay Dirt for chapter 3:

Leaders need to achieve balance in life to be effective. Establishing boundaries is critical for balance and defines the standards and attitudes of a leader. Burnout doesn't have to occur in a leader's life. Good decision-making and abiding by boundaries will enable a leader to function without the angst of being overwhelmed and suffering from low self-esteem.

CHAPTER 4

Do you believe that leading is a personal call?

Every time the phone rang, I grabbed it and answered, "Yes? Anything happening yet?" I was on pins and needles, awaiting news of the birth of our first grandchild. When the call finally came, I was in a hallway between meetings and answered breathlessly. Surely this was The Call! It was. Catelyn Elizabeth arrived with healthy lungs, as I could hear her in the background. My son was beyond excited with the arrival of this precious baby girl.

We've all received calls that brought great joy and calls that brought unwelcome news of loss or tragedy. Calls with bad news aren't wanted, but they come nevertheless. Some of these calls come out of the blue. Even with the advent of caller ID, some undesirable calls can't be avoided, even if we know who it is. Prolonged calls dealing with medical insurance billing or car repairs create anxiety and dread. Because we receive all kinds of calls, we shouldn't be surprised to discover that God is very interested in our response to the call He issues.

Everyone who has lived or is to be born will receive a call—the call to salvation through God's only Son, Jesus Christ. This call is the most important call any of us will ever receive. From God Himself, it is the ultimate call to follow Christ and to live in accordance with His plan for our lives. In addition to salvation, this call includes worshipping God, being His witnesses, and using our spiritual gifts for His glory. While the initial call is universal, many individuals receive another call as well—to ministry and leadership. Jeff Iorg, author of *Is God Calling Me?*, addresses both calls and points out that we must be open to the call to leadership. You may never lead in an official capacity; however, that is not the issue. Let me say it another way: what matters is how we respond when God calls.

Calling is defined as "a strong inner impulse toward a particular course of action especially when accompanied by conviction of divine influence." In *Why Not Women?* authors Loren Cunningham and David Joel Hamilton say this about answering God's call, "When you stand before God, He's not going to ask you, 'What did your family tell you to do? Did you do what your father or mother said? What did your culture say was appropriate? Was everyone happy with your career choice?' No. He'll ask you what you did with what He gave you. He'll ask whether you obeyed His call."

As we consider God's call to ministry, having the support of others is critical. It is unreasonable to expect nonbelievers to understand how He speaks to us and directs us. However, when a man discerns God's call to a preaching ministry, it is almost impossible for him to lead successfully without the support (and call) of his wife. A missionary couple, for instance, that doesn't have a united call, will never be content in an overseas ministry or around the corner in a metropolitan area. I believe God calls couples and blesses their concerted efforts as they seek to live out His perfect will. By the same token, it is extremely difficult for a woman in a leadership role to succeed if she doesn't have the support of her spouse. I'm not saying we must always have everyone's approval and unfailing support before we accept leadership positions. I do believe, however, that when others confirm our calls to lead, their support and understanding make our responsibilities seem more manageable.

The women's leadership surveys revealed a high interest in how effective leaders view their call. Discerning one's call and facing other difficult situations are two specific questions this chapter will attempt to answer. I hope the insights offered by others and Bible passages will help you reflect on what God is calling you to do and how you need to respond to the Holy Spirit's promoting. Consider the following dramatized responses two biblical figures might have had to their call from God to lead.

SERIOUSLY?

"I was living in Midian at the time, tending my father-in-law's sheep. While shepherding one day, I saw something in the distance that intrigued me. As I got closer, I saw something amazing. One of the large blackberry bushes was on fire. The strange thing was that even though it kept burning it wasn't destroyed. That's all I needed on a busy day! I had sheep to tend, herdsmen to watch, and finding water was at the top of my list. I didn't have time to fiddle around with a burning bush!

"If I thought the bush was out of the ordinary, what happened next really unsettled me . . . I heard a voice (pretty quickly I decided it must be God's voice) telling me to take off my sandals because I was on holy ground. I knew that was true because I knew where God is, is a holy place. But I wasn't prepared when God said I was the one He'd chosen to lead the people of Israel out of Egypt. I can't do that! This was not a job I wanted to tackle. He said I'd have help and that with Him all things were possible. I only had to do what He asked me to do.

"If you had time, I'd tell you about what happened when I chose to do things my own way, but that's another story. Knowing now what being a leader would mean for me, I'm not sure I'd have agreed to accept His call. Have you any idea how difficult the Israelites were? Well, I guess you've probably read about it, so you have an inkling of how nothing satisfied them. They were so fickle toward God and in understanding His plan for the nation. Looking back, I see God's plan was masterful, and I realize now it was an honor to be part of all He did for our scraggly bunch. I'm glad I answered His call to lead His people, but believe me, it tried my patience most days. God uses ordinary people to carry out His plans. As long as we follow His directions, we will accomplish extraordinary things." (See Exodus 2; 3; 4; and 12.)

CHAPTER FOUR

I'M NOT JUST A PRETTY FACE!

"For some reason my parents chose to name me Deborah, which means 'honey bee,' so I'm guessing they thought I would be industrious. I've done my best to live up to my name! My husband, Lapidoth, and I complement each other. His name means 'lightning flashes,' so he encourages me in the role God called me to fill. I was perfectly content to work behind the scenes and run our household, but it seems God had other plans for me. As if I didn't have enough to do trying to keep everything ordered, God chose me to be a judge for Israel. Maybe it was my negotiating skills with my children? Or perhaps the counseling times I had with my feuding cousins? At any rate, I sat under a palm tree, and those who needed disputes settled came to me for advice. I tried to be thoughtful in my comments, and when I issued a judgment, I believed I was fair. Lapidoth told me it was because I was a patriot that I answered God's call to be a judge. Being proud of my nation wasn't difficult because I was sure we were God's people and that He was faithful to His promises to guide and protect us. Some time passed and one day Barak, a general in the Israeli army, asked me to accompany him as they fought the Canaanites. Can you believe a military man asked a woman for advice? I know, I was the judge, but this was beyond anything I'd ever heard of! Under God's direction, I told him I'd go into battle with him, but he wouldn't get the credit for the victory. After the Israelites won the battle, I wrote a poem to celebrate. I'd never written anything, so I was surprised that my words seemed to touch everyone. I gave credit to God and praised His name. My people aren't known for their faithfulness; they are always looking around for a better way. I don't know what will happen in the days ahead, but God showed me that when He calls, He takes our abilities and uses them in miraculous ways. So, I'm looked upon as a patriot—and I am. People see me as a God-appointed judge, negotiator, and counselor— and I am. Now they see me as a woman with military experience—and that's true. Some have labeled me a poetess—and I guess I am that too. I'm a ruler also, but more than any of these titles, I'm a woman God called to do things for Him in His name." (See Judges 4 and 5.)

SEEING PATTERNS

When we look at Moses's and Deborah's stories, we can see several emerging patterns. The question most often asked regarding God's call to us is, "How do I know for certain He is calling me and that I can follow it?" When we read the Bible, we see several similarities in all the calls God issued. I believe we can apply the same patterns to our own lives even today. We are mistaken if we think God only calls people to full-time Christian ministry or other major leadership positions. Think about the call(s) you've received from Him through the years. You may work in your home, church, community, or business. Analyze your leadership role, and determine if any of these patterns apply to your situation.

1. *There is an encounter with God:* This may come during Bible study, prayer, or the Holy Spirit's working in your heart. Moses had his encounter with God through a burning bush. Your encounter may not be dramatic like his, but the lack of drama doesn't make the encounter any less real. Most of us recognize an encounter with God, don't we? It may not be an experience we seek, but it will be life-changing when we answer the call. We don't know how God called Deborah, but she must have had questions because becoming a judge was very unusual for a woman. She followed God into new territory, and the result was a healthier and victorious nation.

2. *God gives an assignment that may come in stages:* His call may be to prepare. In fact, in *Is God Calling Me?* Jeff lorg says it well, "A call to lead is always a call to prepare." Moses was to lead the Israelites out of Egypt, and Deborah was to serve as a judge for Israel. Every call from God is unique. Other than the call to trust Jesus as Savior, our calls are as different as our personalities. Educators testify how God called them to teach. Missionaries tell how God called them to share the good news in another nation. Doctors and nurses relate how God called them to use their medical training for His glory. Pastors prepare to preach by attending college and seminary. Every call

involves preparation, which leads to fulfilling the assignment God gives us.

3. *God urges us to accept His call:* Just as He told Moses He would give him helpers to lead the Israelites through the desert, He gave Deborah an extra measure of wisdom, patience, and courage to judge the Israelites during a time they were fighting other nations who wanted control of Israel. Read the assurances of God in Psalms and Proverbs. Both books are full of promises and encouragement. God tells us over and over that if we will follow Him, He will go before us (Isaiah 45:2).

4. *God affirms His call:* When God gives us an assignment, it may be difficult to make a decision to follow His leading even though He encourages us. We may want a complete blueprint at the beginning of our leadership journey. That never arrives, does it? We want to see the results of the trip before we leave! Neither Moses, Deborah, or any biblical personality other than Christ, had full knowledge of what their leadership journey would entail. Moses may not have accepted his call if he'd foreseen how obstinate and fickle his people would be! I'm sure there were days when Deborah shook her head that the people standing under her palm tree didn't have—as my Graney used to say—"sense enough to come in out of the rain!" There's another old saying, "Fear knocked, faith answered; no one was there."

Recently, I checked my emails and found one from a 15-year-old girl I didn't know. She was reading a book on leadership. She politely asked me if I could answer several questions. Her first question was about her call to lead a Bible study at school. She wanted to know how long she should keep doing it. She then asked how to know if God is calling someone into leading women. It was exciting to hear from a young girl already seeking God's guidance for ministry. I wrote back to tell her some of my personal story and to emphasize that one of the best things she could do was to keep asking questions. We have agreed to stay in touch, and I'm looking forward to seeing how God leads her in the months and years ahead.

God's call doesn't just come to polished, accomplished adults. He will work with anyone seeking to glorify His name and engage in ministry.

A PINCH OR A CRUNCH?

Have you ever thought that leading would be easier if you didn't have to deal with people? Difficult situations challenge us, but it's the difficult people we encounter who destroy our confidence. Negativity demoralizes us, and we become enmeshed in fault-finding, criticism, and progress blockades. Sometimes we feel like throwing in the towel. Are you familiar with that expression? It comes from boxing. When the fighter's corner

WHAT OTHERS SAY ABOUT LEADERSHIP

Do these comments match how you approach leading?

"Leaders live in the present, but with one eye fixed on the horizon."
—JEFF IORG, *Seasons of a Leader's Life*

"Our greatest fear should not be of failure but of succeeding at something that doesn't really matter." —ANONYMOUS

"Obedience is the bottom line. Ask yourself: Am I fulfilling the call God has placed on my life? Am I obeying Him in my generation? Am I doing what He has called me to do?"
—LOREN CUNNINGHAM and DAVID JOEL HAMILTON, *Why Not Women?*

"Ministry leading is a calling we answer, not a career we pursue."
—JEFF IORG, *Is God Calling Me?*

"Leadership is not something that is done by people in high places . . . it is done by people in all kinds of roles."
—DAVID COTTRELL, *Leadership . . . Biblically Speaking*

"Leading is tough. Each situation brings its own complexity, and each leader faces unique challenges because of background, temperament, and more." —PAUL TOKUNAGA, *Invitation to Lead*

wanted to avoid further injury in the face of defeat, they would toss a towel into the boxing ring to signal surrender. Likewise, leaders who experience discouraging days and just can't face the opposition any longer may concede the match and give up. Score: opposing side, one; leader, zero.

There is no debate about whether a leader will have to deal with conflict. It isn't a matter of *if*; it's a matter of *when*. My survey revealed there's plenty of conflict to go around! Most of the questions regarding conflict were posed by women in positions of responsibility where their vision and strategies were questioned. I discussed conflict management in great detail in my book, *5 Leadership Essentials for Women*. Leaders must realize there is a difference between conflict management and conflict resolution. All too often, there is no resolution, so management is the only option.

In brief, there are several steps you can take to deal with conflict when it arrives. First, leaders need to anticipate issues that may cause conflict. Be proactive rather than reactive. Be prepared with answers to the hard questions about strategy and direction. Involve others who understand the issues so you have a base of support for your recommendations and actions. Second, as management consultant Bernie Novokowsky said, "Deal with conflict while it's a pinch, not a crunch." Don't let a situation get out of control before addressing it. Step up to your leadership responsibilities, and don't assume someone else will handle the matter for you. Third, remain objective and try not to take disagreements personally, even if you are criticized for your actions and proposals. Sometimes it *will* be personal. An effective leader must stay impartial when possible. If the opposition erupts into a serious battle within your organization or team, you may need to engage a negotiator to manage the conflict.

Is there anything you can do to minimize conflict? It arises in every relationship—at home with your family, at work, with your neighbors, and in your church. Conflict is a reality, and it affects everyone. I've worked on teams where there were differing opinions that caused conflict. I have participated in community events where personality conflicts arose and created tension. One committee meeting I attended sparked a verbal conflict, and one member chose to resign as a result.

You, as the main leader, must maintain a thorough understanding of how to work through conflict. Prepare yourself by learning about those you work with. Answer these questions: What is the purpose, and what are the goals of the group? How much interaction is there between members? Is there competition between them? What patterns do you see when you observe the members?

Figure out how your group learns. Are they visual learners? Do most of them like hands-on activities? Are they good listeners?

DEFINING MOMENTS

When God calls, He wants a response. Whether He speaks from a burning bush in the desert or asks you to trade what's comfortable for a visible leadership role, He focuses on the future, which is His ultimate goal. His timing, like His will, is perfect. We have no idea how perfect His movements are! While we may not spend a lot of time questioning the why or how of His call, we may, however, question why the results of our leading and obedience aren't what we thought they would or should be. One of the best illustrations of this I've ever read tells the story of a missionary couple:

A man and his wife answered God's call to missions service overseas and served God for many years. When they retired and returned to the United States, they noticed a crowd on the airport runway. The husband commented, "Wow! Isn't this nice? A group came to welcome us home!" But as they deplaned, they discovered, much to the man's disappointment, that the crowd was meeting a local celebrity. The waves and cheers were not for the missionaries. This experience really bothered the man, and he became more and more depressed because no one gave them the kind of welcome the celebrity had received. One day, he announced to his wife he was going into the bedroom to pray, and he wasn't coming out until God revealed to him why they hadn't been welcomed home. He was inside for so long that his wife became concerned. Just as she was about to enter the bedroom, the door opened. When he came out, she could tell by the look on his face he'd received an answer from God.

Her husband said, "It's OK. Everything is fine. God told me not to worry because we aren't home yet."

What a powerful example of how God calls, sustains, and provides for us when we obey Him. Even when we deal with conflict, He assures us of His presence and guidance.

DO THIS ONE THING

Look up the following Bible verses, and consider how they address the characteristics of a Christian leader.

1. 2 Corinthians 5:14—We are to be motivated by love.

2. Mark 10:45—We are to serve others as Christ did.

3. Acts 20:20—We are to teach others what they need to know to fulfill their responsibilities.

4. 2 Peter 3:18—We are to be concerned with growing in Christ.

5. 1 Corinthians 9:19–23—We are to be flexible as we lead.

6. Acts 1:8—We are to have God's vision for the world and receive guidance from the Holy Spirit.

7. 2 Timothy 2:15—We are to prepare to lead.

Pay Dirt

Discerning God's call to leadership is preeminent for a successful leader. How a leader deals with conflict will determine how effective she is in carrying out God's assignments. While a leader may receive different calls throughout her life, none is as important as her response to the call to come to God's Son Jesus Christ. Living for Him will bring untold joy and true peace in a world filled with uncertainty and unrest.

CHAPTER 5

---◆---

How does a leader stay close to God?

My husband decided to replace our front doorbell. This wasn't a hasty decision—the bell hadn't worked for years. The picture on the box looked right, and the label said it would install in minutes. Several hours later, we had a hole in the hallway, an opened box on the floor, pieces littering the entry table, and . . . no functioning doorbell. Even when we read the instructions, it often takes several attempts to make things work.

Spiritual growth can be similar. We have God's Word to guide our every step, a perfect manual for living life in the center of His will, but we fail to read it with understanding and don't apply its principles to our leadership lives (or possibly to any other area of lives either). Like a user manual, we must intentionally follow the steps found in God's Word to grow spiritually.

Spiritual growth is an important element of an effective leader's life, which was reflected in how the topic flooded my surveys. Some asked simple questions about Bible study, quiet times, or books on spiritual growth, while others asked more complicated questions, such as how God weaves our experiences into defining moments. I hope this chapter will guide you to a better understanding of how a deeper relationship with Christ can help you be a more effective leader.

Understanding comes through faithful study, reading what God has revealed on the subject, and asking for His guidance to comprehend what we've read. These things—Bible study and prayer—must be present in a leader's life if she wants to grow spiritually. And . . . there's no shortcut to either of them!

BIBLE STUDY

Bible study involves searching the Bible for principles and guidance for everyday life. Just like brushing your teeth and eating vegetables, study must be regular—in other words, a habit, an activity that is established and maintained. Begin with the Bible, and supplement your reading with doctrinally sound resources that put you on a discovery journey and change how you approach problems, deal with difficult people and situations, and relate to family, co-workers, and others. Get a first-rate study Bible, and use a highlighter as you read. When you see cross-references, follow them for a deeper understanding of what the writer intends. *Strong's Concordance* identifies each word in the original language. Knowing how a specific word is used in the text may give you insight into the true meaning. There are free phone apps that enable you to read the Bible in various translations and wherever your day takes you. Bible +1, Logos Bible, and e-Sword are a few examples. Bible commentary apps can help you study. A word of caution here, however: not every commentator on a specific passage will be without bias!

Here are a few passages that talk about the value of knowing God's Word: Psalms 18:30; 33:4; 119:105; Isaiah 40:8; Matthew 4:4; 24:35; 2 Timothy 3:16–17; Hebrews 4:12; and James 1:22.

PRAYER

A pastor asked during a worship service if any of us had prayed enough the prior week. Out of almost 200 people, not a single person raised their hand! We all struggle with praying as much as we feel we should. Pause a moment and ask yourself: Does prayer make any difference in how we carry out our tasks, work with others, or accomplish goals? We are quick to go to others for advice. Are we as quick to humble ourselves, get on our knees, and ask the Perfect Leader how to solve a leadership problem? You may say, "Sure, I do that!" Then why do we often disregard what God says? The Bible has a lot to say about prayer. Jesus is our ultimate role model for how we are to pray—with fervency. Read these verses for a better understanding of the value of prayer to equip you to be an effective leader: 1 Chronicles 16:11; Psalm 145:18; Proverbs 15:29; Matthew 7:11; Romans 8:26; Philippians 4:6; Colossians 4:2; 1 Thessalonians 5:17; James 5:16.

"Love the Lord your God with all your heart and with all your soul and with all your mind" (Matthew 22:37) is a great verse to help us navigate the issues of spiritual growth. Let's consider the verse's three key words: *heart*, *soul*, and *mind*.

+ Heart—Because we don't know how long our lives will be, our hearts must be in a constant state of readiness—ready for God to use, ready for His plan to be lived out, and ready to lead as He wants us to lead. We should want God to find us in the best state of mind possible! If we are faithful in our Bible study and prayers, we'll be in that state of mind.

  Turn to these verses that point out how our hearts are to be aligned with the things of God: Psalms 20:4; 51:10; Proverbs 3:5–6; 4:23; 27:19; Jeremiah 29:11; Romans 12:2.

+ Soul—Matthew 16:26 asks, "What can anyone give in exchange for their soul?" What in our lives will have priority? Where will we place our confidence? On what will we rely? Will we trade eternal peace of mind for the things of life that will fade away like the wildflowers out in the meadow? Our lives may tell a story of the trades we've made as we live without regard to spiritual things, not stopping to consider our sphere of influence as leaders, wives, mothers, neighbors, or fellow believers.

  Here are several passages that might help you realize how important tending to our souls is: Deuteronomy 4:29; Psalms 42:11; 62:1; 63:1; 103:1; Jeremiah 6:16.

+ Mind—God has created us with minds able to achieve things thought to be impossible. Brilliant people have applied their extraordinary minds to mechanics and created inventions that changed the world. Scientists' discoveries came from a curiosity of cell division, growth, and function. One of my favorite television series is about five young adults and a nine-year-old boy with staggering IQs. Each week the team takes on seemingly impossible assignments to save the world, stop corruption, and fight crime. The result is a frantic hour of activity that defies what my poor mind can understand! Reality or fantasy? Well, we have barely tapped the human mind, so who's to say their escapades couldn't happen?

God designed our minds to achieve great things, but the most valuable thing we can do with our finite minds is to delve into the mysterious concept that He, the mighty Creator, wants to be part of our lives. He wants a relationship with us and sent His Son to make that possible. Therefore, we need to use our minds to pursue spiritual things. Paul tells us in Colossians 3:2, "Set your minds on things above, not on earthly things." Some versions say "set your affection," which indicates we choose where our affections lie. What would happen if our focus on spiritual matters were as strong as our attention to other things in life? Would we find ourselves living on a higher spiritual plane? Could we achieve more for Christ? Would we be more effective leaders? Focusing on the things of God will bring greater wisdom and discernment and enable us to face difficulties with God's peace.

Read the following Bible verses, and consider their meaning for your current leadership role(s): Romans 8:6; 12:2; 1 Corinthians 2:16; Philippians 4:7.

> Continual growth is a key to effective leadership, and God is the key to growth.
>
> —LEROY EIMS, *Be a Motivational Leader*

WHAT CAN I DO TO GROW SPIRITUALLY?

John Maxwell, in his book *Leadership 101*, says, "Leadership develops daily, not in a day." Wouldn't it be nice to take a once-a-day spiritual-growth pill? In this day of microwave meals, next-day delivery, and text messaging, we may approach spiritual maturity the same way. To consider spending years studying the Bible and praying for guidance isn't attractive to us. Almost every evening as my mother and I watch television, a question comes up, and I turn to a device to look up the answer. I've learned whether or not celebrities are still alive, about a game show champion's musical history, or if I have the ingredients to make a recipe mentioned on a cooking program. If I had smart appliances, I could bring up an image of the inside of my refrigerator to see if I needed milk, all while standing in the grocery dairy aisle. While we may have moments of sudden insight about passages in the Bible, most of our understanding comes from concentrated study on a specific topic or book of the Bible.

There are many Bible study methods, and each has its own benefit. Your can read the Bible from Genesis through Revelation. Or you can follow a plan that covers the entire Bible within a year, prompting you to switch back and forth reading Scripture from both Old and New Testaments. You could do a topical study. (Servant leadership would be a great topic!) The options are nearly limitless—daily devotional studies, specific word studies, and even chronological studies. Through your study, God will lead you to make changes in your life and apply what you learn about His plan for your life. A large part of this process is having good resources that will help you study.

DOES SERVANT LEADERSHIP MEAN I'LL BE CHOPPING CARROTS?

When our family moved to Cheyenne, Wyoming, we joined a church and became involved in its missions emphasis and ministries. There was a Wednesday evening meal built around missions groups and prayer meetings, and it was an unwritten expectation that every woman would take her turn in the kitchen to help prepare the meal. I've never found much pleasure in cooking but decided this was a way to connect with other women and be a servant leader, so I signed up to help. The menu for that night involved carrots and celery. I spent the entire afternoon chopping and slicing, and I quickly became frustrated with what I deemed as a waste of time. They never asked me to help again (my chopping skills were obviously lacking!), nor did I volunteer. Give me seminars and missions awareness activities—not vegetables!

I met Betty when I moved to southern California from Denver. She served as the Sunday School secretary for our church and was a quiet woman who rarely spoke unless asked a direct question. I never heard her speak in a business meeting, but she was always present. She didn't teach children or sing in the choir. In addition to her Sunday duties, Betty cleaned the church restrooms every week. She'd never been asked to clean them, and she didn't receive pay, although I'm sure on her limited income the extra money would have been useful. For Betty, her job was valuable because it prepared God's house for worship on Sunday. Quietly going about her work, she labored week after week performing menial tasks that most of us were delighted someone *else* did. I moved away from the area a long time before Betty passed away, but I know she continued her labor of love as long as she could. She always comes to my mind as the epitome of a servant leader. Why? Because she was working for her Savior's glory. She did what she did because of her servant attitude.

Wanda Lee, executive director emerita of Woman's Missionary Union®, auxiliary to the Southern Baptist Convention, was interviewed for an article in the missions organization's magazine, *Missions Mosaic*, prior to her retirement. She encouraged leaders to look at their past to see how God's hand has led them. She said, "Leadership is a sacred trust, a spiritual journey to grow and mature in our faith." The issue concluded with an article written by Wanda herself where she stated that leaders can never overcommunicate their message, must establish strong relationships, and serve, leading others to serve.

In his book, the *World's Most Powerful Leadership Principle*, James Hunter defines servant leadership as "influencing people to contribute their hearts, minds, spirits, creativity, and excellence and to give their all for their team." So, then, what comes first—leading or serving? If we lead hoping our efforts will someday point to a servant lifestyle, we might wait a long time! If we set goals and make plans thinking the result will motivate others to serve God, we might be surprised that even though goals are reached, the "heart" hasn't changed.

Leading from a servant's perspective is a heart issue, and our attitudes as leaders will have a tremendous impact on how we approach leadership, relate to others, develop strategies, or face change. A servant leader needs to be TRUE.

T–TRUSTED

A servant leader must be trustworthy. "Show yourself in all respects to be a model of good works, and in your teaching show integrity, dignity" (Titus 2:7 ESV). If you know people who make promises with no intent to keep them, you know trust is hard to give. Be a leader who inspires trust.

R–RESPONSIVE

As leaders, we are to lead—not run over people! A servant leader looks out for the interests of others. Her goals are not the most important thing. She isn't adamant that her plans are the only good ones. Others' opinions matter. While goals, objectives, and plans are important, they are not more important than people. As servant leaders we need to respond to the needs and interests of others. Working with and through a team demonstrates a leader's ability to set aside personal agendas for the good of everyone. The primary goal is to serve the team, group, or organization.

I was blessed to be a member of several churches my father pastored. When he discovered a need, he would discuss it with various people until one of them would stand up in a business meeting and suggest an actionable plan to meet the need. He wanted no credit for the idea; his goal was for the church to work together to accomplish God's will.

> The reason we are on the planet is to serve one another. That is the entire reason for our existence.
>
> —DALAI LAMA

> You will either step forward into growth, or you will step back into safety.
>
> —ABRAHAM MASLOW

U–UNDERSTANDING

A TRUE leader will be open-minded and approachable. People want leaders who are willing to understand others' specific situations. Every situation a leader faces is unique. Being a servant leader is not a one-size-fits-all way of life. Leaders must be flexible enough to understand what is being said between the lines and take appropriate action. An effective leader endeavors to understand participants, issues, and processes.

E—ENERGETIC

Who wants a leader who regards her responsibilities listlessly? Openly invest in projects and activities. Work with enthusiasm and motivate others to serve alongside with the same passion.

Pay Dirt

"Many are the plans in the mind of a man, but it is the purpose of the LORD that will stand" (Proverbs 19:21 ESV). God's plan for us is simple: know Him and live for Him. The responsibility for spiritual growth rests on our shoulders. We can't rely on osmosis, and we can't blame our failure to thrive on anyone else. When we commit to learn about God and His will for our lives, we have taken the first step of a lifelong journey of discovery. As we learn about Him, we will incorporate His principles into our lives and become servant leaders.

◆

How do you build new leaders? Who mentored you, and what did it mean to you?

One Sunday, my husband and I took a couple to lunch after the morning worship service. The wife and I had met several times at women's events, and I knew a little of her background. While we were in the restroom washing our hands, she turned to me and said, "I want to tell you something. I'm giving you permission to mentor me." Because I could see the seriousness of her expression, I didn't laugh or respond immediately. While I am always looking out for potential leaders to mentor, I'll admit this woman was not on my leadership list. She said nothing about what she expected from the mentoring relationship or what she thought she wanted to learn from me. I said very little that day, left matters alone, and waited to see if she followed through with her idea. Time passed, and she never mentioned it again. Whether she had second thoughts, didn't remember what she'd said, or decided she didn't need mentoring, I'll never know. The experience taught me a valuable lesson: it is critical that expectations be expressed and both parties are receptive to a relationship. Nothing positive can come from an association that isn't mutual!

As I read and reread the questions on the women's leadership survey I conducted, I discovered many participants were interested in developing new leaders. The surveys covered a wide variety of women, so the responses covered different interests. This chapter will discuss which qualities leaders should have to be effective mentors. We will also talk about the importance of mentoring others or being mentored. Healthy teams are usually an indication of a leader who is skilled in igniting a passion in others and motivating them to excel for the good of the group or organization.

LEGACY AND INFLUENCE

Who has influenced you the most in your lifetime? In his book, *Leadership 101*, John Maxwell writes about a leader's influence and says, "The true measure of leadership is influence—nothing more, nothing less." Whether or not we realize it, others are observing us as we lead. If we are doing the right things, the right way, it's all to the good. However, if we are poor role models, that will be remembered, and much may not be forgiven!

James 3:13 is an excellent verse for leaders to remember as they seek to be positive role models for effective leading, "Who is wise and understanding among you? Let him show it by their good life, by deeds done in the humility that comes from wisdom." The results of teamwork and goal setting will be more positive if there is a good role model. Leaders cannot underestimate the influence they have on others. Small things like punctuality, printed meeting agendas, or thank-you notes impress others because they represent the leader's depth beyond the trappings of good manners and thoughtfulness. As James states, things done in humility will point to a leader's understanding and empathy.

Most of us can name an individual who has influenced us at a critical time in our lives. It may be a great aunt who raised us, a grandmother who taught us, a Bible teacher who shared God's Word every Sunday, or a missions leader who took us under her wing and modeled what it meant to minister to people in need. Influence is a powerful thing, and leaders need to be mindful that there is always an opportunity to teach and model.

HOW TO BE AN INFLUENCE

Test your influence. Remember: your influence is felt even when you're not intentionally exerting it!

T / F   I don't put a lot of emphasis on my position and focus instead on people.

T / F   I am interested in forming relationships.

T / F   I try to be available to the needs of the members in my group.

T / F   I can list my leadership strengths, and I know my weaknesses.

T / F   I try to keep my attitude positive and approach followers/ co-workers with honesty.

T / F   I am open to change and will be a change agent.

T / F   I see the big picture and focus on leading others into the future.

T / F   I show others how to maintain focus and momentum.

T / F   I am committed to developing new leaders and have a plan to equip them.

T / F   I love to learn new things and model that attitude in my group/ team/organization.

HOW TO ENLIST NEW LEADERS

If you want to ensure your success in enlisting and training new leaders, here are some tips:

1. Take your time as you decide whom to enlist. Not everyone will provide what your team or group needs at a particular time. Consider how her personality, interests, and needs align with the rest of the group.

2. Have a written plan for equipping the new leader. This may include training opportunities, resources they'll need, job descriptions, etc.

3. Evaluate the person's capabilities. Can they handle the responsibilities of the position? When you've done this, let them lead! It's called "learning to fly!"

> Even when you are not paying attention you are influencing other people. Yes, people are watching you—you are always leading. You have no choice about being a role model for others . . . the only choice you have is which role you will model.
>
> —DAVID COTTRELL,
> *Leadership . . . Biblically Speaking*

4. Be committed—training up a new leader isn't a one-hour session!

What attracts people to a group or organization? Could it be that they want to be part of an environment that encourages and supports them? The answer is yes! Individuals want someone to acknowledge their abilities and capability to grow and improve as human beings. They want to participate in something larger.

It is critical for a leader to create a leadership culture. Many times we become so involved in projects and activities that we relegate leadership development to the sidelines. Our organizations cannot thrive if we wait until we have time to think about the leaders we need next year. We cannot wait to see if we receive funds for training before we make plans to equip the fledgling leaders on our teams. If we don't have a definite plan (regardless of any financial issues), we won't have capable leaders to assume new roles in our organizations. A leader can do several things to encourage leadership development:

✓ Regularly provide resources to help skills development
✓ Offer full or partial scholarships to attend training events

✓ Clarify—in writing—what is expected of new leaders
✓ Ask for input based on learning experiences
✓ Assign more difficult jobs to assess new leaders' understanding of the complexity of your organization

Several years ago I was part of a large leadership structure in which each individual trained for a specific role. Drastic budget cuts made it difficult to offer adequate training, so I focused on using my limited funds to the best advantage. Rather than purchasing new books, I found used resources for marginal items and allocated budget dollars to buy yearly curriculum pieces. Unable to pay all travel expenses to training events, I managed to pay registration fees and meals en route. To cut costs, I paid for hotels based on two or three to a room, and the participants made up the difference if they wanted private accommodations. We stretched our limited funds by arranging training sessions in homes and short meetings in hotel rooms to avoid meeting space fees. If we enlist new leaders and don't equip them, we are limiting their effectiveness and hurting our organizations. A great deal of money isn't always necessary to provide leadership development opportunities. Being creative in the face of financial limitation may be the answer.

HOW TO INCREASE YOUR RATE OF SUCCESS WITH NEW LEADERS

Your commitment to developing new leaders must be strong because it takes a lot of energy and a heavy investment of your time, but it is well worth the effort.

To a large degree, your success in enlisting new leaders will depend on how well prepared you are to work with them. You must know your team's needs, but you must also have a plan to equip new members in place before you enlist them. Did I say this before? I'm pretty sure I have! Your team or organization may have so many needs you can't focus on one thing. However, if you want to be successful in enlisting and equipping new leaders, your focus must be laser sharp. Here are several questions to ask yourself as you begin seeking new leaders:

✦ What area burdens you the most?

✦ What one person would you like to develop or reach this year?

✦ What will be the greatest barrier to equipping this person?

✦ What one thing can you do to benefit them the most?

✦ What skills do you need to learn in order to train someone else?

> Every time you develop a leader, you make a difference in the world. And if you develop leaders who take what they've learned and use it to develop other leaders, there's no telling what kind of an impact you'll have or how long that impact will last.
>
> —JOHN MAXWELL,
> *The 5 Levels of Leadership*

Draw a picture of an effective leader, or make a list of qualities you expect in an effective leader. Does your drawing or list reflect the type of leader you've become? Does it reflect the kind of leader you want on your team? If you know what you are looking for, the likelihood of finding her or him is greater. Go in with a plan!

———

I bought a new sewing machine several years ago because my old one wouldn't do the job anymore. The salesperson in the store told me the machine came with a guarantee, but it would not be valid if I didn't attend an orientation class offered in the store. I thought that was ridiculous because I'd been sewing a long time! Once I looked at the instruction manual, however, I quickly realized I'd never figure out the intricacies of the new machine without help. So, I made arrangements to attend the class, and with the personal touch of an instructor, I mastered threading the machine, using the attachments, and taking advantage of all the new things the machine could do. I left the store confident I could use my high-tech machine.

The mentoring process is similar to my sewing machine class! The instructor knew what she was doing, and I could watch her work my machine. The hands-on part of the class was great because I could learn by doing things myself with someone close by to supervise. That's where the value of mentoring comes in. A mentor relationship is part instruction and part demonstration. It's guidance by someone patient and thorough. Another part of mentoring is seeing patterns in things. As an experienced leader, you might have forgotten some of the leadership patterns in your group or organization. Without thinking about them, you are used to doing certain things that are foreign to someone new. The patterns you know and see are valuable pieces of information that you should pass on to a new leader.

I have an awesome cat whose personality has brightened our household. Melkie is the only cat I've ever owned who has behavioral patterns. There's no other way to describe his actions! He loves to play games and has a certain routine he follows when he plays hide-and-seek or hides behind the pillows on my bed. His morning pattern right now is to stretch out to his full 30-inch length on the floor while I do my back exercises. He has four felt mice on elastic strings he carries all over the house. He lines them up in the upstairs hallway or arranges them in a circle on my mother's bedroom carpet. There's no doubt he's one of the smartest cats in the Western hemisphere!

All of us have patterns, don't we? It should come as no surprise that the pattern principle applies to our leadership lives too. The mentoring process provides an outlet for teaching patterns (substitute the word *principles* if you wish). Now, I'm not taking about perpetuating outdated patterns. We do enough of that as it is! Using outmoded methodology guarantees an organization's demise. No pattern is worth preserving if it harms the purpose of a worthy effort. We all have patterns that determine our daily behavior. What I'm talking about are actions or behavior beyond mere habit; I'm concerned with the unnamed procedures, agendas, and methods that can frustrate a new leader unaware of the dynamics at work. As we train leaders, we can help them avoid a lot of confusion and aggravation by explaining the history and purpose

> Every generation is strategic.
> —BILLY GRAHAM

behind specific activities. Any time we can relieve tension and facilitate interaction, we have done a good job!

Mentoring is too important in successful leadership to leave to chance. Just as a mentoring relationship isn't automatically healthy, a mentoring plan doesn't happen automatically or accidentally. As the mentor, you need to have a specific mindset to be effective in the relationship. A mentee (the one being mentored) has expectations just as the mentor does. Consider this mentor mindset:

✓ See the big picture as you mentor.
✓ Understand the value of broadening the base of your leadership.
✓ Choose your mentees carefully, and let them know you expect commitment from them.
✓ Be open with them about purpose, strategies, methods, finances, personnel, etc.

VALUE OF MENTORING

So, you're embarking on the mentoring journey! There are several things you should remember when developing your plan of action. First, be up front about the time commitment a mentoring relationship will take. Even if you are mentoring volunteers, there will be some financial outlays; be certain you allow funding for training, attending events, etc. Second, define the purpose of the mentoring relationship. State your expectations and desired outcome. Third, determine how you will address the mentee's needs. Every new leader will be different, so it's important to address her individual interests, needs, and passions. Last, you must be committed to the mentoring process. Make a short list of what you will commit to do for the mentee because this will speak to your commitment and show that you have thought things through.

Will all of this just fall into place? Not necessarily! A large part of the success of a mentoring relationship rests squarely on the shoulders of the more experienced leader, the mentor. You need to be passionate about developing new leaders and see what they will add to your group or team. Seek out creative ways to teach them to lead and grow as leaders. A visionary leader will inspire others to learn and will create in them a desire to be part of something exciting. Communication is a critical element in a good mentoring relationship and is a constant need. As your confidence in the mentee grows and you see progress in their skill development, give them more complex assignments and offer feedback on their performance. Show mentees the value of teamwork, and model a cooperative and positive attitude.

I received a phone call one day from a leader who was in a quandary about a potential leader in her area. She did not know the woman well and was hesitant to bring her onto her team without some background information. I knew the woman and advised she be placed on the team temporarily with a specific assignment, which would help determine future participation. This was a sound plan that enabled the team leader to observe the woman in action without possible serious consequences should her assignment not be completed. Time passed, and another call informed me that the potential leader didn't follow through with the assignment. She abandoned it because she felt it had no value. We need to be careful here as there is no unimportant role on a team, is there? My friend saw, without harm to her team, that this individual would not be a good addition to her team. If you are going to evaluate a potential leader in this matter, make sure the prospect has the skills, gifts, and personality that are the best fit.

> The function of leadership is to produce more leaders, not more followers.
>
> —RALPH NADER

KEY WORDS IN A MENTORING RELATIONSHIP

Do these words describe you? These are qualities and skills you need as you enter a mentoring relationship.

Trust	Expertise in certain areas
Honesty	Experience
Integrity	Commitment
Availability	Passion
Effectiveness	Learner

BETTER THAN QUOTES

Al Capone's attorney, Easy Eddie, garnered his nickname from his ability to get his client out of legal trouble. Time passed, and Eddie had a son. While Eddie offered his son the best things of life, he realized what he couldn't offer—a good example. He turned evidence over to the authorities and eventually testified against the Mob. Within a year, Eddie was gunned down on the streets of Chicago. A few years later, during World War II, a young Air Force pilot on a bombing mission realized he didn't have enough fuel for the mission and had to return to the aircraft carrier. As he neared the carrier, he saw Japanese planes coming in to attack. Knowing his ship was unprotected, as all the planes had been deployed on mission, he fought off the attack and saved those on board. Awarded the Medal of Honor, his hometown named its airport after him. Chicago's O'Hare Airport bears his name—Easy Eddie's son! In his new life, Easy Eddie was a father who mentored his son, and the result was a young man willing to fight for his country, an example for others.

AS YOU MENTOR

Your effectiveness as a mentor will be observed by others. Consider the following to help you become influential in your mentoring relationships.

Every mentoring relationship should involve participation on a team of some type. That should be part of your plan! You can learn a lot about a new leader's personality and abilities when they are challenged by group dynamics and working with different and even difficult people. It will be to your advantage as a leader—and to the success of your organization—if you understand the mechanics of team building. You may be a leader who believes she can do it all. You can't! And, even if you could, you shouldn't! You may not be skilled in delegating, but that's something you need to learn so you can teach it to those new leaders. Are strong teams important in your work? If you lead a missions group at your church, a team of volunteers will help you plan and carry out events. If you are a supervisor at work, you have been assigned to a team.

Most organizations have teams that divide the work in order to more effectively achieve their goals. Regardless of your leadership role, knowing how to build a strong team will be to your advantage. Consider these things as you think about who you will ask to serve with you:

1. **Build a diverse team:** Age, ethnicity, experiences, and backgrounds should be varied.

2. **Don't be in a hurry as you build your team:** Figure out which abilities the team needs and how members will work together. Proceed slowly and choose wisely.

3. **Evaluate the members' abilities and skills:** This will enable you to delegate, make assignments, and form subteams.

4. **Establish a communication process:** Communication must be clear, frequent, sensitive, and open. Let the team know you expect to be informed.

5. **Set measurable goals:** A team is no place for cloudy procedures or muddied communication.

6. **Show your appreciation.**

Teams have a place in all successful organizations. As people work together, they accomplish much more than they could dream of doing alone. See if you can identify what the following teams did:

Lewis and Clark

Fred Astaire and Ginger Rogers

Orville and Wilbur Wright

Currier and Ives

Barnum and Bailey

Rodgers and Hammerstein

Siskel and Ebert

The Dream Team

Paul and Silas

Abbott and Costello

MOTIVATING YOUR TEAM

Several questions on the women's leadership survey showed that some leaders were experiencing difficulties motivating their teams to do the work they needed accomplished. There are basic mechanics of team building, but the cohesiveness of the team doesn't depend on techniques alone. There is a hard-to-define chemistry in successful teams. Leaders who want strong teams should focus on creating team spirit so that when difficulties come (and the will come!), the commonalities they have strengthened will be what carries the team through. Consideration for others needs to be engrained in the group. It is the leader's responsibility to model behavior that is sensitive and uplifting. Motivating each team member must happen before the team can move forward.

When we saw the need for new leaders, a co-worker and I launched a leadership training emphasis. I delegated the training activities to her, and it was interesting to watch her mold a group of women who didn't know each other into a well-oiled machine. They worked together because they shared a passion for equipping new leaders. Because she was creative—one activity included building a bridge out of newspapers, rubber bands, and Styrofoam cups—there was much laughter and fun as they learned! The foyer of our large meeting facility will never be the same!

DO THIS ONE THING

Reflect on the leaders who have impressed you. They could be current or past leaders, family or church members, or others with whom you have a relationship. Write out a few of their leadership attributes. What do you think their counsel would be about your current mentoring and team-building efforts?

If we are interested in leaving legacies that speak to our passions, there are things we must step up and do. Mentoring is not an optional activity that can be done when we feel like it, when we have time, when our schedules are more open. That special relationship occurs only when two people are honest about their expectations and needs and work together to refine their skills. Team building needs to be on every leader's to-do list. Again, it is the best way to accomplish goals and to equip others to lead. A team can be a proving ground for a novice leader to test her wings in a friendly environment.

How do you motivate others to participate and lead?

"All hat, no cattle" is an old expression that was used to describe people who wore a cowboy's fashions but had no experience on the ranch. Their cowboy outfits looked nice and fit well, but there was no personal know-how of roping a steer or breaking a bronco! This person may pick and choose the aspects of a lifestyle that appeals to them while not actually embodying the lifestyle as a whole.

Sometimes leaders can get away with talking the talk without walking the walk. We know what we must do to sustain a close relationship with God and remain in the center of His will. However—and this is a big however—we don't do what is plainly expressed in His Word. That's how we become counterfeit Christians, or should I say counterfeit Christian leaders? The same can be said of leaders who know the principles of good leadership but don't put them into practice. I heard a pastor talk about all the seminar binders and conference notes most of us have. They sit on our shelves and represent knowledge we have not applied. He was trying to motivate us to take action and use what we said we've learned.

Leaders make speeches and lead workshops about enlisting women to join our groups and organizations. We write articles and blogs about engaging women to participate in ministry projects and assuming leadership responsibilities of their own. We become proficient in carrying out the "telling" and often never put those concepts or principles into action ourselves.

When I retired from a demanding leadership position, I realized I could participate in activities that hadn't been possible when I maintained a heavy travel schedule. Faced with working through some of the issues I had talked to women about for years as they struggled to be effective leaders in their churches, workplaces, and communities, now I was on the front line. Would all I had taught about leadership be proven wrong when I went to apply the principles? Was all I'd taught really useful? Did I have the hat, but no cattle? I was about to find out!

In a little more than four years, I felt I had indeed gone through the fire that I'd heard other women mention. Through my involvement in my church and region, I found the leadership principles I had learned as a young woman, honed as I studied leadership as an academic, and applied to train and lead large groups still worked at the local level. The concepts proved correct, but the work was *difficult*. I realized the questions posed over and over again on my women's leadership survey were real-life ones. The issues they faced in enlisting, engaging, and motivating others were real and important to leaders, regardless of their positions.

So, here are some of the questions that relate to motivation. I will spend the majority of this chapter discussing the elements of motivation and the leader's approach to moving others toward spiritual growth, ministry involvement, and developing their leadership skills.

✦ How can you get others excited and enlist their participation?

✦ How do you get others to serve with you?

✦ How do you inspire others to adopt your vision and follow your lead?

✦ What forms of motivation do you find most effective?

✦ What are some creative ways to sustain interest?

✦ What techniques do you use to empower those you lead?

✦ What motivates you even through the tough times?

✦ What do you do to be encouraged when you're feeling defeated?

Whew! This is quite a list, isn't it? The common element in all of these queries relates to motivation. Many times the leader is the sole driving force in the beginning. The leader needs to be skilled at creating an atmosphere that ignites interest and enthusiasm in others. Her vision and energy will help groups develop goals and do the work.

I believe there are two areas of motivation that determine how successful a leader will be in the complicated process of enlisting new members and their development as future leaders: What motivates you as a leader? And, how do you motivate others? Rather than beginning with how you can motivate others, I'd like to start by discussing how you personally stay motivated. If you feel underappreciated or lack the energy to lead, you won't be successful in motivating others to engage in ministry, participate in activities your group sponsors, or embrace the goals you've set.

WHAT MOTIVATES YOU AS A LEADER?

Years ago at a seminar I heard a woman share about her early days in a direct sales company. Her mentor told her, "Even if you don't have any appointments, get up, get dressed, and go out the door!" Nineteen years later she was still doing that, and her annual sales were in the $250,000 bracket even though she was living in a small town. While we may find it easy to motivate others, motivating ourselves may be difficult, especially if we haven't practiced self-starting all our lives. We ask ourselves, "Is it worth it?" "Does all of this really matter?" "Who cares other than me?"

One of my supervisors, a quiet man and a deep thinker, covered the walls of his office with framed motivational posters. I sat in his office many times and read and reread the quotes he displayed. While he wasn't a powerful speaker, he had a commanding presence and was always there to help me reach my organization's goals. There were very few times I left his office unchallenged to do a better job, unmotivated to stretch myself beyond my perceived limits, or lacking new ideas of how to improve my organization. While we can't rely solely on framed posters to motivate us, we can take some of them to heart.

And we as Christians know there is no substitute for the practicality and sound instructions we receive from reading and studying God's precepts. Recalling some Scripture will strengthen our resolve, and it can help us be more precise in our approach to motivating others and ourselves to perform with excellence.

There is no shortage of information about how to stay motivated! Visit the Internet, and you'll see what I mean. Salespeople and supervisors around the world read motivation manuals, articles, and devour volumes about how to motivate themselves and their employees. Pastors often struggle to motivate their congregations week after week to stay strong in God's Word and seek His will for their lives. Leaders spend hours developing strategies they hope will result in changed attitudes, improved techniques, and increased results.

But what happens when leaders themselves struggle to find their own motivation? This question was asked so many times in my women's leadership survey that I realized it was a topic that took priority even over leadership skills. Following are four steps you can take to ensure you are operating under motivation and not by rote. We often become so familiar with our processes and goal setting, we fall into a rut. No one is inspired to do well. No one is encouraging others to participate. When this happens, the original purpose is lost, and members begin to ask, "Why do we do this?" "Why do it this way?" "Who cares?" If this is happening in your group or organization, it's time to step back and reassess your approach to leading. Perhaps we are the one who needs a change! Attend a conference with a fresh approach to leadership, or take an online seminar or two.

SIX STEPS TO STAYING MOTIVATED

1. Evaluate Your Emotions
Little is done that doesn't engage our emotions. You may feel you failed to lead your followers to embrace a new project, one you believed vital to the future of the group. How were you feeling when you presented this new opportunity for involvement? Were you dealing with family issues, or had you been passed over for a promotion at work? Had you exchanged words with a neighbor that left you wounded and weary?

Feelings of despair, anger, bitterness, frustration, or low self-esteem can undermine your attempts to motivate others. Multiple disappointments may hit all at one time, and together they can become too heavy a load to carry. Thoughts of stepping aside as the group's leader can result in a presentation that lacks the impetus it deserves.

Don't fool yourself by thinking your emotions won't be detected by others. They may not show on your face, but they will come out in other ways. Our emotions affect our motivation.

2. Stay Positive

If you are positive in your approach to your leadership responsibilities (even though they may get you down sometimes), your "can-do" level will be higher. Staying positive brings increased productivity.

3. Remember

Good memories can do a lot to encourage you and spur you on to accomplishing other things for your group or organization. When you find yourself sinking into a mire of self-pity and having feelings of inadequacy, it's time to recall better times when your efforts were met with enthusiasm and productivity. If you are working on strategy and nothing is coming together, take a break at your favorite coffee shop or go for a walk in the park. Of course, the caffeine may help! If your feelings persist, it may be an indication that something is amiss physically. A vacation may be what the doctor orders.

4. Stick to the Basics

When overwhelmed by the complexity of a situation, focus on basic leadership responsibilities: learn to let go; break down your work into manageable pieces; set daily, weekly, and monthly goals; establish routines; and avoid procrastination. To sustain momentum is difficult when we are discouraged, but staying motivated (even in doing the humdrum outer trappings of leadership) can help carry a leader through difficult times.

5. Rely on Others

If you don't have a mentor, find one, and use their suggestions or strengths to move you forward.

6. Evaluate Criticism

Your critics *may* be right, at least in part! If necessary, take action to remedy or change the situation that caused the criticism. A response to critics should not be postponed. A leader must constantly evaluate purpose and direction and be ready to change direction and do something entirely new if the situation demands it.

Perhaps now you see there is hope for you as a leader! God does not put us on a shelf when situations become difficult. He wants to use us, and He provides what we need through the presence of His Holy Spirit and encouragement from His Word and by especially gifting us to do what He asks of us. He also sends others to help navigate the riptides of leadership. If you still feel adrift, make an appointment with an experienced leader you respect, and talk about how they deal with lack of personal motivation. Trust me—every leader faces instances when the responsibilities loom larger than life and when it takes too much energy to move, let alone lead.

HOW DO YOU MOTIVATE OTHERS?

Now that we've discussed motivating ourselves, let's talk about motivating others. Leaders are responsible for enlisting participants to become part of our groups and organizations. Once they've joined (for whatever reason), we must motivate them to participate. They will be more likely to participate if the activities themselves have value to them. Remember some of these new members are your future leaders! This task is a tremendous one because of the sheer amount of time it requires.

How in the world do we create enough enthusiasm and interest to attract someone to the degree that they want to be a part of what we are trying to do? And then, after enlisting them, we are expected to get them to participate? What an assignment!

My family and I were members of a medium-sized church years ago. I loved to sing, so I was active in the adult choir. One couple came to choir practice and eventually joined the church, but we never saw them at any other functions. They came to practice and services—that's all. It didn't take long to surmise they joined the choir, not the church! We tried to enlist them for Bible study, missions activities, and fellowship events but were never able to motivate them to participate beyond that initial point. They admitted to several leaders that other than music, tennis was their life focus. Numbers shouldn't be the focus; active involvement of every member should be our goal.

RECIPE FOR SUCCESS IN MOTIVATION

1. Encourage Others
Individuals are more content and perform better when they know someone appreciates their actions and recognizes the value they add to the group or organization. Encourage others by praying for them, checking on them, and helping them lead through difficult situations.

2. Create Excitement
When excitement is generated as part of your challenge, you encourage creativity and growth opportunities. People are more likely to join when their sense of adventure is activated.

3. Communicate, Communicate, Communicate
Remember that communication—constant communication in many forms—is critical in the motivation process. Leaders who fail to communicate fail to motivate.

4. Know Your Team
Recognize that real motivation comes from within and only grows in fertile soil. Learn what is important to those you are trying to motivate. Discover their interests, and let them know you are available to help. Individuals' personal goals may motivate them to participate.

5. Provide Continuing Training

Training promotes growth experiences and is an important element in motivating the connection within the group or organization. Give individuals under your care tools to do their jobs! (Reread chapter 6 on equipping leaders.)

As you develop a strategy for motivating others to work with you, it is important to evaluate how skillful you are in presenting the need for their help, why you want them to join the cause or effort, and how they can help. No one has the time to attend meaningless meetings. I don't know about you, but when I set aside time to attend a meeting or gathering, I want to feel my time was not wasted, my input was valued, and that I either learned something new or was challenged to do something. When this doesn't happen, I get nervous future activities or meetings will be the same. And I don't have time for that! I may be retired, but my time is valuable!

In light of all women do today, leaders have a tremendous responsibility to take their schedules into consideration. Most leadership books will give you a list of things to do to make your meetings productive. Your local library and online sources will be helpful. My book *5 Leadership Essentials for Women* is a comprehensive resource with practical suggestions for managing time, communicating, and working through conflict to build strong, effective groups.

> To succeed . . . you need to find something to hold on to, something to motivate you, something to inspire you.
> —TONY DORSETT,
> 1976 Heisman Trophy winner

> Motivation is the art of getting people to do what you want them to do because they want to do it.
> —DWIGHT D. EISENHOWER

> I believe it's clear . . . crystal clear . . . that people are attracted to and retained by institutions that make them feel good about themselves as human beings.
> —TOM PETERS, *Leadership*

ASSESS YOUR MOTIVATING SKILLS

Take a few moments and complete the following assessment to determine how strong your motivating skills are

+ Are you an effective communicator, or do you find it is easier to keep people in the dark?

+ Do you reward others' contributions to your group or organization? List five ways you do this.

+ What types of contributions has your organization made? What types of recognitions has your organization received?

+ Do you give direction, support, and feedback to those you are trying to motivate? How do you show your support?

+ What do you do when someone under your leadership takes on new duties? How do you follow through?

+ Do you provide the skills training your followers need to do their jobs? How?

+ How creative are you in motivating others to join, perform, and excel? List some of the things you've done.

+ Are your team members satisfied with their accomplishments? How do you foster positive feelings in this area?

There's a lot of pressure to perform, isn't there? Leaders complete tasks, create goals, and develop strategies. Now we are expected to keep followers motivated too? That's a lot to ask! There is no shortage of checklists to help a leader develop skills that result in healthy groups with strong members who are motivated to perform with excellence.

You may ask, "Does it ever end?" I'm sorry, but the answer is no. As author Bob Adams said in *The Everything Leadership Book*, "Motivating [others] is an ongoing process because people are continually growing and changing." How we motivate others to join, participate, and stay engaged in community projects, missions-related activities, or neighborhood endeavors will say a lot about our general leadership abilities. None of this comes naturally; it takes work and determination on our part.

LEADERSHIP CHECKLIST

Take a moment to look over the following list of what leaders do. Rate yourself on a scale of 1 to 5, with 5 being you do this often and 1 being you don't do this at all. If any of them are missing in your leadership life, it might be a good thing to read some of the resources cited at the back of this book to become a more informed, creative leader.

I . . .

Create opportunities	1	2	3	4	5
Say, "I don't know"	1	2	3	4	5
Develop talent	1	2	3	4	5
Am a visionary	1	2	3	4	5
Know when to wait	1	2	3	4	5
Am optimistic	1	2	3	4	5
Convey a grand design	1	2	3	4	5
Attend to details	1	2	3	4	5
Work to break down barriers	1	2	3	4	5
Nurture new leaders	1	2	3	4	5
Develop trust	1	2	3	4	5
Am a relationship expert	1	2	3	4	5
Develop networks	1	2	3	4	5
Am a lifetime learner	1	2	3	4	5
Know myself	1	2	3	4	5

Accept responsibility	1	2	3	4	5
Stay focused	1	2	3	4	5
Express my passion	1	2	3	4	5
Communicate constantly	1	2	3	4	5
Have high regard for personal integrity	1	2	3	4	5
Possess a servant's heart	1	2	3	4	5

Now that you've had the opportunity to evaluate your skills related to motivation, let's look at motivating others to engage in ministry, enlisting and training new, younger leaders, and evaluating how a leader's ideas, actions, and activities can motivate others to become involved.

A WORD TO MINISTRY-RELATED LEADERS

People participate in groups for various reasons. What attracts them to your group, project, or organization is seldom your winning personality or outstanding articulation of need. More often it is something related to *their* personal interests and needs. They may be drawn to your organization because they see action taking place, and they like that aspect of the project or group. But remember, they may have no desire to work against obstacles.

This last statement may be a new thought for you. Not everyone is interested in being part of an organization that spends its time arguing about traditions or discussing who isn't aligned with the organization's purpose. I've found this to be especially true of younger women. Is this a reason many women do not join various religious-oriented groups? A group locked in a 1969 mindset does not appeal to people in Generations Z, Y, X, or even baby boomers. We overdiscuss to combat apathy, "us vs. them," or other barriers to service, and this can keep younger women from joining in our good organization. The women outside your organization want enjoyment from participation. A sense of victory isn't something that motivates them unless it's related to doing a job with excellence.

PRACTICAL, APPEALING, OUT OF THE ORDINARY

I have always been an avid reader. While fiction is my first choice, I read many interesting books in search of new ideas to apply to my leadership roles. Several years ago, a new leadership position challenged me to attempt new things to increase women's involvement in ministry and missions. As I found new approaches to enlisting women of all ages, I discovered there were new ideas around every corner! Not every idea is usable, however. I began a long-term search for creative ways to attract women to join others in reaching around the world with the love of Christ by praying for missions efforts and giving financially.

Any person searching for creative ways to accomplish a goal and step forward as an effective leader will discover she is limited only by her notion of what is acceptable. Every leader must cross real or imagined barriers. In 2 Corinthians 5:13–14, Paul says he had done some things in his life that might appear crazy to others but that he'd done them because of his love for the things of Christ. God gave us inquisitive minds, and it's a shame when we set aside the unusual and untried in favor of the accepted and proven.

While speaking at a recent women's retreat I put several items in sacks and divided the group for an activity. Each woman was to draw an item from the sack and brainstorm for a new ministry project. My instructions were, "I want fresh ideas! If you have a ball of yarn, do not say you'll make lap blankets for a convalescent facility!" Once women began to think outside the box, their responses were refreshing as they thought of new ways to minister to those in need.

Caution: If this is uncomfortable for you—good! Read books on creative thinking, and see how you can apply them to the work you do. Two I've found to be particularly helpful in this area are *Jump Start Your Brain* by Doug Hall and *A Whack on the Side of the Head* by Roger von Oech.

So, how can you use your God-given abilities to motivate others to join your movement, group, or organization? I've chosen three broad categories where we try to motivate others to join us: engaging new leaders, recruiting younger women, and putting ideas into action.

ENGAGING NEW LEADERS

Where are the new leaders? Are they sitting at a desk in your office or on a couch in your Bible study group? Do they attend the same community events as you? Do they live next door to you? If you don't look around and pay attention to others, you'll never find them!

If you are seeking someone to mentor as a new leader for your organization, look for someone who stands out either in her personality or by her actions. It is not unusual to select someone for a leadership role because we have seen them functioning in another position of responsibility. You may have heard someone talking about a woman who has shown organizational skills that would benefit your group. Observe her, and pay attention to how others respond to her. Find out what experiences she's had in leadership. A seasoned leader could be standing right next to you!

However seasoned she might be, it is likely she will require training and orientation to work in your organization. You must—yes, *must*—have a plan to equip and prepare women to lead regardless of the role they'll fill. Our family was once in a church with a large children's ministry. The buses owned by the church transported large numbers of children to church every week. Unfortunately, the church did not have sufficient space or trained teachers to cope with the children. They herded the children inside, closed the door, and left one person to handle them all alone. How much teaching happened? Not a lot. Needless to say, good leaders were few and far between.

The same thing can happen in our organizations when we enlist leaders but fail to prepare them. Develop a specific strategy to train women to become effective leaders in your organization. Please . . . don't spend only 20 minutes with them to put them in the loop. That is not training!

Training is also a high indicator of how successful your motivation attempts will be. Don't believe for a minute how you train new leaders will go unnoticed! If you are thorough in your training, your new leaders will feel confident in their assigned roles, fulfill their duties, and stay with you. If you are specific in your expectations, they will understand the organization's goals and the processes they need to follow.

What are your plans for new leaders? Throw them in a room and shut the door? Here are a few ideas for innovative training:

✓ **Host a New Leader Tea:** Use this informal gathering to present an overview of your organization and its purposes and goals. Participants can meet current leaders. (Why not ask two of them to tell about why they enjoy participating in your organization?) Plan for plenty of time for meeting, greeting, and of course eating!

✓ **Create an Attractive Printed or Digital Piece:** Provide information to serve as a reference guide about the group or organization. Keep it brief, and post it to your website or email it to potential leaders.

✓ **Utilize Available Online Training:** Woman's Missionary Union® has multiple online courses for leaders of different missions education age levels as well as some general leadership courses. Visit wmu.com/training for more information. The cost is minimal, and the courses are new and interactive.

✓ **Recognize Leaders:** Encouraging current leaders will show new leaders that their work will be appreciated. If possible, invite prospective leaders to any recognition events so they can see your team's camaraderie.

✓ **Provide Leadership Resources:** New Hope Publishers has published several books that are good resources for equipping new leaders, including *TeamsWork* by Joyce Mitchell and my books, *5 Leadership Essentials for Women* and *Awaken the Leader in You*.

RECRUITING YOUNGER WOMEN

When you focus on enlisting new leaders from a younger generation, there are several things you should consider. Anytime an older leader seeks younger women to fill leadership roles within an organization, she may see herself standing on the edge of a deep ravine with her target women on the other side! Some women can successfully span the wide differences, while others may flounder. To move in a world of women in a different generation from you may be as much of a culture shock as a trip overseas!

For instance, I was once part of a missions trip to Croatia where we had been asked to offer leadership training for an emerging leadership team. This team of women had no previous training. In fact, one woman told us this was the first time she had been asked to share her opinion! Our youngest team member spoke about motivating younger women to attend missions events and participate in missions-related activities. She shared how her church got younger women involved by having a pajama party at the church where they painted each other's nails while studying leadership skills development. The American ended by saying, "After all, it isn't the 1800s!"

Prior to our trip, our team leader had given us background material that included information about how their culture was still emerging from civil strife and oppression. Actually, it almost was the 1800s for the Croatian women, who were recovering from civil war and religious persecution. I shuddered and heard our team leader mutter, "I can't believe she said that! They may not listen to anything we have to say after this."

But we simply did not give these enthusiastic young women enough credit. We moved through the rest of our presentations, suggesting the women take small steps, while considering women's interests and values. At the final wrap-up session, the Croatian women shared what the training had meant to them. Her eyes sparkling, one woman said, "And, we'll begin buying new pajamas for our special event!" They moved past the faux pas to embrace a new idea. Another Croatian woman commented, "We've heard some of these things before, but you've given us wings to fly!" That was exactly what God had called us to do at that point in time!

Those of us who have held leadership positions for long periods of time and have had a variety of positions need to be thoughtful in how we attempt to motivate younger women to join us as members or leaders. We cannot use the same techniques past leaders found successful. So much has changed for women younger than 40, and to be successful in enlisting and equipping future leaders, we need to know of the shifts that have occurred. It is similar to navigating another nation's culture!

Here are several suggestions that might help motivate younger women to assume leadership roles in your group. Keep in mind that learning about cultural shifts will mean adapting your approach, methods, and attitude.

TEACH LEADERSHIP SKILLS

Adapt the skills to different age groups. Creativity is prime property for younger women. For example, if you equip a new leader with information about the history, purpose, and goals of your organization, be prepared that she may use new terminology that resonates with her generation as she presents the same information to her peers. I saw this happen in person at a women's training conference. We had enlisted a young woman to lead a seminar about our organization and its tasks. We were surprised—and delighted—as she told the attendees all about the organization in fresh, glowing terms that brought smiles to the faces of her audience. Her presentation put the organization in a new light! It was refreshing and attractive to other young women, and she had in no way diluted the message.

LOOK AROUND YOU!

Take into consideration your new leaders' life situations—their families, work life, and obligations. While you must not misrepresent the time commitment your leadership position will take, your positive approach and experience can show younger women that the purpose and results outweigh the effort.

As you try to motivate others to join your cause, create experiences for them that feature multisensory experiences. The atmosphere— sounds, smells, and don't forget the tastes!—can all be utilized to create an inviting experience. Now hear this: *the days of sitting in a large circle with no outer stimulation are gone!* Visit a new church that seeks to engage young adults, and you may find vastly different styles of music and worship. It may not be what you are used to or even what you prefer, but remember you want to motivate younger women to take part. So take a deep breath and try something new!

You may be largely engaged in leadership opportunities within a church setting. While the suggestions in this book apply to that venue, by no means are they limited to church life. I attended a community event to raise funds for its senior citizen programs. The venue, a school, was transformed with colorful lights, decorated tables, live music, and tasty food from local businesses. The atmosphere was conducive to quiet conversations, and anticipation built as we bid on baskets donated by individuals and businesses. While the planning committee tried to create an event that would be attractive to younger adults and included younger vendors in the event, very few attendees were younger than 55 years of age. I'm not sure if younger adults helped plan the event, but that would have been one way to encourage all ages to attend. In addition to involving younger adults in planning, make sure everyone understands the value of the event.

HANDS-ON

Focus on the going rather than just the sending. This has been a topic of long discussions among leaders. To motivate others to become leaders is not easy work, but it can be very rewarding when you see an increased participation that will make your organization healthier and more productive. Younger women are busy, but when they see the value of your purpose, they carve out time to participate. You inspire them by showing how valuable and rewarding the hands-on experience can be.

The other day I saw a poster online that caught my eye. In fact, I liked it so much I bought it and am waiting for it to arrive! The poster was a world map with the continents formed from fingerprints. The quote was, "Be sure to leave your mark on the world." Isn't that exactly what we are challenging others to do? Let their work—their hands—make a difference?

Whether you are a missions leader, a community volunteer, a non-profit employee, or a leader in the workplace, leaving a positive mark on the world is a worthy aspiration. This illustration speaks to the attitude of many younger women. Show them why your group or organization matters, and they may be motivated to become involved. You can lead them to see that their involvement is important and that much of it is hands-on.

Once you have enlisted a younger woman to take a leadership position and begun training and equipping her to fulfill her responsibilities, I have one further word of advice: guide, don't dictate. The quickest way to lose a young woman is to demand strict observance to the way she does her job. Allow her to be creative, and don't dictate the "how." I was standing next to an older leader when a young woman approached her to volunteer to lead a new group of younger women interested in missions. My older friend looked her right in the eyes and said, "Of course you can. As long as you do it the right way!" Ever see fire dim in someone's eyes? That's what I saw happen in a matter of moments!

Doug Hall, in his book *Jump Start Your Brain*, encourages businesses to be creative in their marketing and in training their teams. His point is that people don't buy "things"; they buy intangibles. I've replaced his words with my own to illustrate the same idea to remind leaders to focus on the intangible aspects of leading.

✦ Don't sell me process. *Sell me purpose.*
✦ Don't sell me obligation. *Sell me commitment.*
✦ Don't sell me tradition. *Sell me innovation.*
✦ Don't sell me "must." *Sell me "let's."*
✦ Don't sell me hurry. *Sell me preparation.*

PUTTING IDEAS INTO ACTION

It begins with you. You must stay motivated yourself. Motivating others to participate and perform with excellence requires a lot of your effort and time. It is a rare thing (write it down if it happens!) for a leader to

walk into a group, make a plea for new leaders, and leave
a list of more volunteers than she needs. Because this alr
pens, it is difficult to remain motivated and positive. Un
couragement overflows into our planning processes and is manifested in
what we try to do for our groups. The lower we sink into negativity, the
less likely it is that actions and activities will be successful.

So, how can we as leaders stay upbeat as we plan? Is there a formula
for successful activities? I'm sorry to say there isn't. If there is a formula, I
haven't found it. And believe me—I've looked! What we can do, however,
is gather our teams, committees, and members and develop a strategy
that will maximize our efforts. At the end of the day (or week, month, or
year), we want to look back and point to some positive forward movement
and results. Make sure the group's goals are being met. The results might
be increased donations, volunteers, sales, or trained personnel. Whether
you lead a marketing team, write sales manuals, direct a women's shelter,
or work through an agency to provide services to immigrants, motivation
is key not only to adding to the membership rosters but also to being successful in expanding your ministry, influence, and efficiency.

Several years ago, the Woman's Missionary Union published a book
titled *I Can Do That! 100+ Ways to Be on Mission*. I received a copy and
glanced through it, thinking at the time it would be a good resource for
someone new to a missions-related leadership position. I bought several
more copies and gave them as gifts to pastors and interested persons.
The overall response was, "Where has this been? These are great, easy-
to-do ideas we can use!" The book was a simplified statement of ideas
that experienced leaders had been using for years. But . . . it had been
packaged differently and was user-friendly! The book was an entry point
for many who had not walked through the door of missions involvement before. That's what we must do to keep people motivated to join
in our activities and to take action as we seek to serve together in the
workplace, community, neighborhood, or church. Our actions as leaders should move our groups and teams forward and increase their efficiency, numbers, and influence.

Did you know Ben Franklin wrote under a penname? He published the yearly *Poor Richard's Almanac* under the name Richard Saunders. Through his penname Franklin said, "You double your odds of success when you stick out your neck and do something different," and also wrote a version of "Humpty Dumpty Sat on a Wall," which I think says more than I could in several pages:

> New and Different sat on a wall,
> New and Different had a great fall.
> All the King's horses
> And all the King's men
> Proceeded to put them together again.
> Giving New a new tweak, starting Different from seed,
> Doing the New and the Different is how you succeed.

LAST THOUGHTS ON MOTIVATION

It would be wonderful if we, as leaders, could maintain a positive outlook all the time! When goals aren't met or numbers decrease, it's difficult to motivate ourselves, let alone others, to join our efforts. Motivation is one of the trickiest things a leader has to do. We all know how important motivation is. Successful motivation keeps an organization viable. It's how goals are met and people respond to challenges. People are motivated by many things: greed, money, relationships, fame, and jealousy. But they are also motivated by a desire for peace of mind, personal growth, goodwill, and, if they are believers, by the Holy Spirit's guiding hand.

When you accepted your current leadership position, you probably didn't think too hard about the role motivation would play in your success. That's the "sweat of our brow" part of leadership. It demands we exhibit positivity, creativity, and endurance. There is no way we can motivate others if we ourselves aren't focused or innovative. We must be students of human nature and learn to decipher the motives of those we are trying to influence.

Motivation is a natural leveler. By that, I mean all of us need to be motivated. If you are the CEO of your own company or serve as chairperson of a community agency, you have to remain driven to invest in the future. In your position as coordinator of a nonprofit organization or the lead member of a task force at work, it's critical to motivate others to work with you. Leaders face many challenges, none more difficult than staying personally motivated and stirring others to action.

Whether you are fighting to stay motivated yourself or to move others to relate to your group's purpose, remember what Richard Saunders said, "The only way to get a significantly different result is to do something significantly different."

How do I become an effective leader?

ock and load" is a military term referring to a soldier's need to be pre-pared for immediate battle by making sure the weapon is ready—not unlike how leaders should approach their leadership roles. Because there were so many survey questions about leadership skills, this chapter will discuss training and specific skills that help leaders be effective. To facilitate the discussions, I've used some of the actual questions and will respond to them one at a time.

There is no way to overemphasize the importance of being prepared. There will be times when your preparation is the only thing that stands between you and failure. When you invest time and energy in learning how to do something, the results will be beyond your wildest dreams. You may have already thought through which sections you'll skip in this chapter. Or maybe you'll read an entire book on communication. There is always one more thing to learn! One section of John Maxwell's book, *Leadership 101*, is entitled, "To Lead Tomorrow, Learn Today." This is so true!

You may question the value of attending another leadership sem-inar, but it could provide you with one bit of information that helps move your group, team, or organization to the next level of productivity you've been struggling to reach. If the members of your team or group lack training, it is your responsibility to see they receive training. Your budget may be limited, but if you make training a priority, the results will outweigh the financial investment. If you assume a leadership position in a period where no training is being offered, don't wait until it is offered again to equip those with whom you are working. Even if you must lead the training yourself, it will be worth your efforts.

Years ago I worked with a large volunteer team. Their experiences varied, there were age differences, and not every member's first language was English. It was a challenge to teach each of them the skills necessary to do their jobs. I established basic criteria, and as new members joined, I gave each one a packet of information with which they were to become familiar. The most important pieces were about the history and purpose of our organization along with a set of books I wanted them to read. Because our team was the hub from which we did all our work, I had high expectations for each member. I sent out a monthly newsletter outlining events, upcoming dates, and deadlines for projects. As I read articles and found new resources, I sent updates and summaries of information I'd read in addition to planning their formal training.

I've said all of this to impress upon you the importance of training those with whom you work, even if they are volunteers. The success of your group will directly relate to how much emphasis you place on preparation. In chapter 7, I mentioned that my family had been members of a church that became heavily involved in a bus ministry that grew beyond its means, which ended up overloading the teachers. While the purchase and maintenance of the buses was a financial drain on the church, the staff was committed to the ministry, so they kept it going. Workers for the bus routes were enlisted and trained, and the buses rolled out every Sunday morning to bring several hundred children to Bible study and worship.

The problem was there had been little preparation to care for the unaccompanied children once they arrived at the church. I learned from one Sunday School teacher that the bus driver would usher 30 children into her room, large enough for about half that number, and leave her alone with them! Experienced Sunday School workers dropped out in droves, and the bus ministry almost ceased to exist. All because the church leaders did not make adequate preparation, provide proper facilities, or enlist and train enough workers to care for the children.

We are sometimes overwhelmed by all we have to accomplish, and training is often set aside for a more convenient day and bigger budget. But the problem is there is rarely a more convenient day and seldom an adequate budget to provide all the training needed. My bottom-line advice is this: Develop a detailed training plan for your organization and provide resources, encouragement, and learning opportunities for everyone on your team. If you encounter resistance from supervisors or bosses, present the value of the training via a workable and realistic training plan.

RAISE YOUR HAND IF YOU HAVE A QUESTION

The women's leadership survey revealed many questions about communication, delegation, public speaking, and skills development. Let's look at some of them.

COMMUNICATION

What are the most effective means of communicating?
Today we can communicate easier and faster, but the challenge of accurate, clear communication is still with us. We can send a confusing email before we check it for clarity. Inaccurately reading between the lines is possible with an email too. And don't even think about text messaging! My texting shorthand is a huge joke with my family, so I am careful with abbreviations and phonetics. I think I've communicated when in actuality, nothing has made sense in my recipients' eyes! Whether you communicate face-to-face, via telephone, email, texting, formal letters, memos, reports, or PowerPoint presentations, be careful that what you say is what you mean. Anticipate questions and try to answer as many of them as you can in your first communication.

Word of caution: don't tell everything you know in your communication. Keep it short but informative. If you need something from the recipient, be precise in what you need. It is

> Listening is the leader's secret weapon.
> —JO OWEN, *The Leadership Skills Handbook*

critical your communication is timely and accurate. Be motivating, rather than negative. No one wants to only get only bad news from the leader! When possible, save criticism for private, face-to-face meetings.

How do I minister and communicate with language groups?
The first thing you must do if you lead language teams is to gain a basic understanding of their culture. There are some excellent resources to help you learn about other cultures. I've listed a few of my favorites. Observing customs and cultural manners is an element you must build into your training emphasis.
+ *Cross-Cultural Connections*
     by Duane Elmer
+ *Geography of Time*
     by Robert Levine
+ *More Than Serving Tea*
     edited by Nikki Toyama and Tracey Gee
+ *Faces in the Crowd*
     by Donna S. Thomas

How do I conquer my fear of public speaking?
I don't know that anyone ever gets over the nerves associated with speaking to a large group! As much speaking as I've done for the past 20 years, I still feel a tremble of nerves as I get up to speak. Knowing your audience is critical as the information will either relax you or put you on your toes. There is no substitute for preparation when you are speaking to a group of any size. Winging it is not acceptable! You need to have practiced enough so you can glance at your notes and move smoothly from point to point. One of the best books I've ever read on this subject is *Speak Up with Confidence* by Carol Kent. She approaches this topic with practical suggestions, and if you follow them, you will not be paralyzed with fear as you speak.

> Perception may not be real. But the consequences of perceptions are real.
> —JO OWEN, *The Leadership Skills Handbook*

DELEGATION

Which responsibilities do I keep, and which do I pass on to others?
Take a few moments to list your current leadership responsibilities. Categorize and prioritize them. Indicate the ones you can delegate to someone else. Then, do it! Journal your current leadership responsibilities, and refer to them often to check on your progress.

As you look at the lists you've made, you may need to train others before you can delegate the tasks. All too often leaders try to lighten their load and make assignments with no thought to whether the individual can perform the task. Look back over your lists. Are there items that do not align with your organization's purpose? If you find some that are marginal, reassess their value, and meet with your supervisor to see if he or she will reassign those projects or functions.

Have you worked with a team steeped in tradition? The committee or group may try to carry duties that have little connection or relevance to its original purpose. They continue because "it's always been done that way." I have inherited several of these groups. I guess, at one time, the methods had value, but all I could see was the wasted time and energy. The old guard is in place to see that the traditions are maintained. After sitting through numerous poorly prepared and delivered presentations and seeing no connection between speaker and audience, at the next meeting, I used the allocated time for activities that were more interactive and informative. No one questioned my changes, and I think I heard a collective sigh of relief!

You can't do it all yourself, and you don't want to because you don't build leaders that way, so you must delegate assignments. But delegation takes work! A leader must think strategically, establishing priorities, and assigning duties. Delegation can't be done on the spur of the moment. The functions of a group, team, or organization are important to its success, and you need the right person to perform each specific duty. Assigning a project to the wrong team member can mean disaster. I once delegated responsibilities to two women who were each talented, capable, and ready to accept the assignment. While they had distinct responsibilities, they needed to work together. Time passed, and I assumed (never do that!) their work was progressing well. But when I asked for a report, there were murmured replies to the effect, "I haven't done anything on that yet." I couldn't understand what had happened—or what had not happened! After months, I discovered the problem: seemingly, the two women couldn't work well together, and I'm not sure they even liked each other very much. It was a hard lesson to learn. I thought I'd done my homework, assessed preferences, and matched their abilities and interests before I delegated responsibilities. Even when we do our best, not all delegation will be successful.

Regroup, plan again, reevaluate, and keep delegating! Delegation is a leadership skill you must have in your arsenal of abilities. Remember it is your responsibility to see your assignments are carried out! You can't delegate this important responsibility to someone else.

How do I delegate effectively?

Once a leader gets past any issues with control, she is ready to delegate. It's difficult to give someone else part of your authority, isn't it? Delegation can be a powerful tool to help multiply your efforts and effectiveness. However, reaching full potential is what's it's all about, right?

Here are a few ideas about being a successful delegator:

1. Decide what needs to be done and who can do it.

2. Determine how important each task is and how it fits into the group's vision and purpose.

3. Answer these questions: What are the standards for the work? When is the deadline? What will happen if deadlines aren't met or work isn't completed?

4. When making assignments, give the individuals the authority they need to complete the task.

5. Be specific about how you will support the person (resources, financial help, etc.).

It is important to communicate your reasons behind delegation. Keep purpose and vision before them. Successful delegation will encourage creativity and develop leaders.

PREPARATION AND TRAINING

Even while distributing my women's leadership survey, I sometimes underestimated women's interest in leadership development. For example, at a women's retreat, the women who gathered around tables munching candy and nuts comprised a diverse group. There were young women, one with a nursing baby, retired women, and everyone else in between. The majority was interested in the survey and what they could do to prepare themselves to lead. I don't think any had aspirations to be CEOs of a company, but they recognized that to fulfill any leadership role, they needed to develop skills. It was refreshing and encouraging to see evidence of an interest in learning.

It's all in the preparation! It doesn't matter what your responsibilities are. Whether or not you hold a titled leadership position and manage enormous amounts of money isn't the issue. The issue is how well you learn skills that help you be an effective leader.

What qualities should I prioritize as a leader?
First, being prepared means you want to learn. There must be a curiosity about the next new book to read or training seminar to attend.

Second, effective communication is a must in a leader's life. If a person has difficulty communicating, problems are sure to follow! Writing and speaking are leadership skills for which there are no substitutes.

Third, a good leader needs to learn to be organized. This is a learned skill so everyone can excel at organization. There is no excuse for a leader's life to be a mess of missed appointments, unmet deadlines, or half-completed projects.

How can I develop leadership skills?

Simply put: you can't fake expertise! If you have an assignment at work, it is your responsibility to discover what you need to know to complete it. That might involve interviewing someone or attending a seminar. Maybe even reading the dreaded manual! You may accept a volunteer position for a community event only to discover you are clueless about what you need to do. Read through reports to find out the history of the event. Talk to people who've been involved before. If you can delegate, gather as much information as you can, and organize actions to ensure assignments are carried out. To fulfill your responsibility you may need to train others. This may involve learning yourself. Staying informed will help you understand your assignment and reach goals.

Your employer may send you to a training seminar to learn how to do your new job. Perhaps your church has an annual equipping event. There may be orientations available in your community or through county agencies. Training is available for nearly everything anyone will ask you to do, so take advantage of it! Don't rely on the skills you've developed in other areas because those skills may not apply. If you've accepted a volunteer position, training may be more difficult to get. That's where the Internet becomes your best friend! Search for assessments, reports, statistics, courses, and overviews that may equip you. Many are available for free.

To a large extent how conscientious you are as a learner will determine how effective you are as a leader. You know the old saying, "You can lead a horse to water, but you can't make it drink." Even though there is a multitude of learning opportunities available, when leaders think they are too busy to attend a training seminar, they are trying to take shortcuts. Leaders are never through learning and must be committed to the group's purpose to put forth the effort to continue learning. Skills development comes step by step.

What is the last book you've read and can recommend?

In the appendix, I've provided a list of books I've found particularly helpful. Take a look and start reading! The fact is, there should be a book on leadership on a table or chair somewhere in your home. Leaders must be learners—and that means they must read.

Start reading!

If I'm in charge of training my group, how do I begin?
A Japanese emperor commissioned an artist to paint birds. Months passed and then years, and there was no word from the artist. The emperor finally went to the artist for an explanation. When the artist put a canvas on his easel and painted a bird in less than an hour, the ruler asked why the artist had taken so long. Leaving the room, the artist returned with his arms full of drawings of feathers, wings, heads, and feet. Extensive research was necessary to complete the painting.

This is a wonderful illustration of how a leader is to focus on preparation. It is vital that a leader focuses on keeping motivation high (see chapter 7) so that group members and new leaders understand the value of what they are doing. If you, the leader, don't have a plan to equip your followers, you will be singing the blues sooner than later! Don't assume group members know or understand the goals or vision. What you are trying to do may be new to them. They may have no frame of reference. Emily Morrison, author of *Leadership Skills*, said, "The way people feel affects their conduct more than the way they think." What's that got to do with preparation, you ask?

Consider this scenario: As group leader you haven't taken the time to familiarize your members on the group's history, purpose, or goals. You are so busy you haven't focused on each member's duties and how they relate to the whole. Who do you think will pay for your neglect? Both you and the group. When we fail to equip those under our care, we damage relationships, stifle creativity, delay progress, and decrease results and productivity. You must plan to prevent these destructive things from happening.

What can I do to help my group/organization fulfill its purpose? How can I plan and overcome obstacles that would hold us back?
The British sculptor Sir Jacob Epstein had a writer visit his studio. The

writer noticed a massive block of marble and asked what it was going to be. "I don't know yet. I'm still making plans." The writer seemed surprised, "You mean you plan your work? Why, I change my mind several times a day!" To this the sculptor replied, "That's all very well when you're working with a four-ounce manuscript but not with a four-ton block of marble."

Leaders must develop a leadership skills plan for their organization. You may have inherited a budget that has no provision for training leaders. If that is the case, then it's up to you to provide opportunities for members to learn leadership skills. How? Let me give you some personal examples.

When I was leading a team of both experienced and new leaders, I had little money to pay registration fees, lodging, and travel required for training events. Because I believed training was essential to the well-being of our organization, I made plans to lead essential training myself whenever we met as a team. This included at least 30 minutes for a workshop on a leadership topic. I prepared handouts, assembled folders, copied articles, and provided everything for them, while explaining what results I expected from our brief time together. Over time we covered such topics as reporting, communication, time management, working with church staffs, planning events, and the basics of conference leading. When possible, another team member who had special expertise led that training portion of our meeting.

Some years I offered a leadership retreat. We would cram as much into the time as possible. If the keynote speaker could come early, I used her expertise to lead a training session. We didn't always have nice meeting facilities, but if I had to use my hotel room, that's what I did. In order to equip leaders, I used every available moment to train them. On occasion, I asked team members to arrive early for an event so we could spend a brief time for leadership development. My husband and I had two extra bedrooms in our home, so some stayed with us to save expenses, and my husband, an excellent cook, prepared fabulous meals that cost little compared to restaurant dining or catering. I became an expert in no-frills training!

When possible, I ordered used books from websites that had free or reduced shipping. The members of my team didn't mind using gently worn materials, and it enabled me to maximize my budget. Over time I learned to realign budget line items and allocate more funds for leadership development. When I sent team members to an event, I asked them to attend as many seminars as possible and to work out a schedule so there was little duplication among team members. When we met the next time, they prepared a presentation of what they learned so everyone could benefit from the training. This stretched my budget for maximum affect. Over time, our team became a group of generalists, and each member was cross-trained. That way they could substitute for each other, and it was great for our effectiveness!

The women I worked with were so committed to growing as leaders they even sometimes funded portions of their own training. If you initiate this method, however, do be considerate of women who may not be able to contribute. Whenever financial difficulties prevented a woman from attending a conference, I arranged a scholarship for her. Key leaders *must* be trained. No excuses! Make a plan! Train them.

As always, talk to other leaders to find out how they approach training new and experienced leaders.

Not long ago while on a business trip, I stopped in a coffee shop. I noticed a mural on a wall that told the story of how coffee is grown. The hand-lettered labels showed how the grower tested the soil nutrients before planting. Isn't that what a leader does as she seeks potential new leaders? She knows the soil and climate for growth and lets that knowledge guide her as she prepares to enlist and equip new workers.

The coffee tree doesn't bear for the first three or four years, so coffee is a long-term investment for the farmer. The largest drawing on the mural had labels pointing out

> If you have an apple and I have an apple and we exchange these apples, then you and I will each have one apple. But if you have an idea and I have an idea and we exchange these ideas, then each of us will have two ideas.
>
> —GEORGE BERNARD SHAW

the inner leaves (the oldest), the midleaves (mature), and the outer leaves (younger). This is a wonderful picture of how teams should grow: the oldest leaves (experienced members) are there to protect, the mature leaves (less advanced members) offer shelter and experience, while the light green leaves (new team members) are visible and keep the tree viable.

Drawn in the middle of the mural was a row of coffee trees with a row of shade trees behind them. My initial thought was the larger trees were there to protect the younger coffee trees, similar to how experienced leaders protect younger ones while they develop their skills. When I returned to my hometown coffee shop and talked to the manager, his eyes lit up when I asked him about the shade trees. "Actually," he said, "the trees weren't planted to shade the shorter coffee trees, but the workers! I saw this firsthand in Costa Rica where my company sent me for training (*ah . . . leadership training!*). The farmer knew he had to attract seasonal workers to his farm. They are free to go to the farm that is the most attractive to them, so shade trees gave him an edge for returning coffee workers! Isn't that a key element in attracting leaders? Create an atmosphere where learning is exciting, training is creative and ongoing. And where new leaders are welcomed, you'll have a "farm" where workers will return year after year!

See? Learning about leadership can take place anywhere. Even in a coffee shop!

CHANGE

How do I initiate change when it is needed?
Oh, the heated discussions that have taken place over proposed changes! Gallons of coffee are consumed, voices are raised, agitated hands gesticulated, and heads are sure to shake! A leader who makes organizational changes must be a brave person. You may have had that joyous experience and told yourself you'll never do it again. In fact, many leaders have fallen because of change. I took a graduate course entitled "Implementing Positive Change," and it was an interesting preview of all that can happen when an unprepared leader tries to navigate the stormy tides of change.

Have you thought about how the traditions we value have undergone change over time? Traditions are important things we aren't willing to set aside—the much-loved and revered processes and the familiar approaches to problem solving, structure, or ministry, which have held us in their firm grasp. Is change always about moving away from proven methods and the familiar? Absolutely not! However, there may be indications your team's effectiveness has plateaued and is no longer performing at its highest level. That old status quo has surfaced again and is keeping your group from attracting new members and potential leaders.

How those under your leadership embrace change may depend on your ability to remain positive and approachable during a transitional period. If you resist change, your group will catch your attitude. If you refuse to initiate change or implement others' decisions, your effectiveness may end. If your leadership position is at work, you may be in danger of being labeled "uncooperative" or "unable to adapt." You might find yourself looking for a new job!

A leader of volunteers might have more input concerning change than someone in a paid situation. Working on a community project with your neighbors may give you greater freedom to initiate change rather than carrying out someone else's ideas and decisions passed down by management. Regardless of your position, if you can't embrace change, you will be left in the past! Leaders can't afford to be satisfied with things as they are. They must approach leading with enthusiasm, optimism, creativity, and minimal fear of change.

Reading this section may cause you to think about your leadership responsibilities in your family. Perhaps you homeschool your children. Do changes occur in those roles? Of course. We make career adjustments, relocate to new cities, and experience financial and relational changes. Change is a given; it is with us in every area of our lives.

Here are several tips that might help you move toward implementing positive change:

> Improve your own leadership ability by striving to stay one step ahead of the change cycles.
> —SHEILA MURRAY BETHEL,
> *Women in Leadership: Daily Devotions to Guide Today's Leading Women*

1. **Learn about what the proposed changes will involve.** Who will be affected? Will there be a timeline? What are the benefits of the changes? What is the negative side of the changes?

2. **Determine your course of action.** Be prepared to answer a lot of questions, and don't be insulted when they are probing or negative.

3. **Develop a strong strategy for implementing the changes.** Make assignments, communicate frequently, enlist the help of persons who favor the changes, set deadlines for specific actions, and keep everyone informed.

4. **There is no such thing as overcommunicating.** People want to know everything about anything that affects them.

How do I deal with negative behaviors and stubborn mindsets in the midst of change?

First, leaders need to remember that some things should never change. A leader's commitment to God and His principles should never change. When situations arise that contradict biblical mandates, leaders must stand firm in their convictions, not wavering even in the face of possible reprisals.

Cartoonist Ashleigh Brilliant said it well, "Agree with me now; it will save so much time." Leaders spend countless hours trying to get followers, employees, co-workers, fellow volunteers, and family members to embrace coming changes that will affect their relationships, job descriptions, income, or even their location. It is the leader's responsibility to show others the benefits to change. When we fear change, our resistance is often disproportionate to the actual change that occurs. In other words, we overreact!

Do you remember the television series *Monk*? The detective suffered from multiple phobias that caused his life to be a never-ending series of obsessive actions. He had a long list of things he feared, and they greatly affected his daily life.

Look at this list of phobias, and see if you know what they are. If not, look them up.

✦ Chronomentrophobia (It may be time to change.) *fear of clocks*
✦ Pentheraphobia (You'll get a kick out of this one!) *fear of mother-in-law*
✦ Xanthophobia (Beware of spring.) *fear of color + word yellow*
✦ Blennophobia (Don't have any little boys!) *fear of slime*

None of us like the unknown, and change brings fear as we wonder what it will mean for us as groups or individuals. Did you know, however, that fear can motivate us? Lee Colan, in *7 Moments That Define Excellent Leaders*, says the word *fear* can stand for "False Evidence Appearing Real." And, isn't he right? We hear about coming change and leap to worst-case scenarios. We are so distraught that all movement and actions cease. Leaders must help others move beyond their initial refusal to accept the proposed changes. An effective leader prepares answers to questions and has accurate information to diffuse volatile reactions to change.

If you must lead your group through change, you'll need to examine your own reactions to the change. Be honest with yourself about what you fear. It'll be best if you anticipate others' responses rather than waiting for them to come to you. Help others see that we may miss wonderful opportunities by not accepting, embracing, and implementing change.

Several years ago, the leaders of Baptist women in Croatia requested a training team to come help members develop their leadership potential. Coming out of a civil war, many women had suffered great loss—loved ones and homes—and carried the scars of change only war can bring. They did not view themselves as leaders. As our team planned workshops to address basic leadership skills, it soon became obvious we were asking them to do things beyond anything they'd ever done before! Each of us led workshops that best matched our personalities and careers, hoping we would make better connections with the women. We tried to be flexible and make our sessions interactive. Hundreds of Croatian women attended the final event where we lead breakout sessions. The topics were announced, but no one moved. We passed through the audience to encourage the women to move to the designated areas for the workshops. They weren't being uncooperative; they'd just never had choices for small-group learning and didn't know what to do. Fear of the unknown kept them in their seats. Once they attended the sessions (with more prodding!), they loved the small group discussions and the topics we'd designed to help them grow and realize that they too could become leaders.

How do I work through the challenge of change?

Change can be beneficial. Without change an organization will stagnate and become ineffective. Change can bring creativity and fresh perspectives; however, if you are leading change in your corporation, at church, in a community project, or even at home, you may see little or no reaction to the change proposal. Does that mean everyone is on board with the changes? Not likely! They may think the change won't affect them, or they don't want to make waves. Whatever reasons keep them from asking questions and responding can be unhealthy. As the leader, you should know the answers to these questions:

1. Do they understand what the change(s) will mean for them, the group/team/organization?

2. Have they dismissed what you have said?

3. Are they uncaring?

4. Why are they so hesitant to discuss the changes?

5. Have they been through changes that have been ineffective?

> In times of change, learners inherit the earth, while the learned find themselves beautifully equipped to deal with a world that no longer exists.
> —ERIC HOFFER

> We must always change, renew, rejuvenate ourselves; otherwise we harden.
> —JOHANN WOLFGANG VON GOETHE

A leader never needs more courage than when leading change! Read what others have said about leading change, and record how each one relates to your current leadership position.

PRIORITIES

How do you prioritize?

Show me a leader who doesn't prioritize, and I'll show you a leader who is disorganized, unfocused, and pulling out her hair! Rick Warren said it right: "It is usually meaningless work, not overwork, that wears us down, saps our strength, and robs our joy." This is true, isn't it? I can look back to times when I was overwhelmed and see much of what I was doing had minimal impact when applied to the larger tasks I had. In other words, I was wasting time and energy on things that weren't critical to achieving organizational goals or purpose. Now we're back to that old conundrum of determining what is urgent and what is important.

Who establishes your priorities? You! Others may dictate the "what," but only you can set the standards for how you work. You and no one else make the decisions for much of your activity. My women's leadership surveys revealed a high interest in learning how to prioritize leadership responsibilities for maximum influence. This was of interest to younger and older women alike. Their position and responsibility didn't seem to matter. Leaders questioned their ability to make sound decisions regarding the use of their energy, time, and abilities. In light of that, here are a few suggestions that might help you set priorities for your work and life.

✓ Make a list of your assignments, and note deadlines.

✓ Divide the list into four smaller lists (by day, week, or other category).

✓ Group activities that relate to a specific event or task.

✓ Establish initial priorities by assigning each category (or item) a number.

✓ Determine which items or categories are critical, which are urgent (the deadline is tomorrow!), and which are important (the walls won't collapse if they aren't done by 5:00 today).

✓ Estimate how long each task will take, and make a note next to the deadline.

✓ Begin with #1 and work through your list.

You have just established some priorities! This will work for personal activities as well as leadership responsibilities. Will there be interruptions? Of course. Will your timeframe be too short? Probably. But at least you now have a guide to effectively move toward reaching goals, developing skills, and feeling good about your daily accomplishments.

What role does the spiritual play in how I establish priorities? How do I maintain spiritual sensitivity, power, and perspective?
Mark 9:23 (ESV) says, "All things are possible for one who believes." In Matthew 17:20 (ESV) we read, "If you have faith like a grain of mustard seed, you will say to this mountain, 'Move from here to there,' and it will move, and nothing will be impossible for you." We find assurance in Matthew 11:28, "Come to me, all you who are weary and burdened, and I will give you rest." These three verses promise us that when we turn to God, He will guide us and equip us to do what we previously labeled as impossible.

A desire to set priorities is a positive step toward creating balance. When our lives are more ordered, we are more confident and effective. When balance comes from looking to God for His direction, it is even sweeter because of its Source! In her book, *Knit Together*, Debbie Macomber writes about how she believes we will have a greater chance to have balanced lives if we always put God first.

All the leadership techniques (while they help us) aren't as important as our worldview. Our attitude and outlook affect setting priorities more than the external issues such as organization and goals. How we look at the world will influence our priorities. I know a young woman who uses God's Word to establish priorities for her career and family. How she manages her time comes from God's principles about using her days to honor Him. She approaches her career as a means to glorify God in what her students learn. Having made the decision regarding spiritual priorities early in her married life, she is imparting those insights to her family and in the workplace. Navigating the intricacies of priorities with God beside her at every turn, she doesn't wake up in the morning wondering what her priorities will be that day.

Pay Dirt

Growing as a leader is complicated. Being an effective leader is even more difficult! Leaders must wear a large tool belt that holds the skills of delegation, change implementation, communication, preparation and training, and priorities. If any of these tools is missing, the leader is in trouble!

CHAPTER 9

---◆---

How do you make time for yourself?

The words *juggle*, *manage*, *stay on track*, and *coordinate* appeared numerous times in my women's leadership surveys. Time management is still at the top of many women's lists. This chapter takes a practical approach to focus, goals, and organization. Because time management invades every area of life, I believe discussing these issues together will help women be more effective leaders.

I think my daughter inherited my list-making gene. After an extremely busy time as she assumed more responsibilities in her music education career, she began texting me when an event or activity was over with a single word: *check*. Especially near the holidays or at the end of the school term, I received the same message multiple times. *Check, check, check!* The concerts, choir competitions, state events, and school musicals consumed hours of her time. Her check system helped her see progress and was encouraging to both of us since I function as an unofficial choir mom. After all, I'm the mom of the director! That makes me the choir mom, doesn't it?

How we manage our time determines how effectively we lead. You may coordinate a community event or lead a youth missions group. Both require an expenditure of time, and if you are disorganized, the hours will tally higher than they need to. If your employer has given you a deadline for a group presentation, time management is critical for a worthy product. All leaders have assignments, goals, and deadlines, even if they are self-imposed. What should be our primary purpose in managing our time? What Jesus prayed to His Father in John 17:4 says it well, "I have brought you glory on earth by finishing the work you gave me to do."

NOTHING NEW UNDER THE SUN

Questions about how we use our time surface every day. There's rarely a conversation between two people that doesn't mention the fleeting hours, short days, or the passing of years. Here are a few from the surveys:

Q: How do you manage your time and get it all done?

A: Of course, you never get it all done!

Q: What is your key to effective time management?

A: I make those all-important lists, categorize things to be done, give each a priority, insert some easy-to-accomplish activities on the list, and then get ready, set, go!

Q: Do you feel you have to sacrifice work to spend time with family? Or sacrifice family to get your work done?

A: If your priorities, goals, and objectives are in place and you let them guide you, you will accomplish more in less time because you aren't wasting energy and time trying to decide which things are more important than the others.

CHANGE FOR TIME'S SAKE

Do you flinch at that word *change*? (If so, reread chapter 8.) I sometimes joke that I'm in favor of change as long as it's others who need to change and not me. As leaders make even minor changes (adjustments) in the way they use time, they will discover processes will often move more smoothly, and they will accomplish more in the same amount of time. How can that be true? Small adjustments in schedules can be the difference between being a frazzled leader and one who (at least on the outside) appears to be in control of issues, leading forward movement. Let's consider some of these changes that can alter the way we lead.

❏ **Evaluate how you currently allocate your time:** Do you pay a high cost for the way you use your time? Do your choices create positive situations? If not, change something today.

❏ **Look at your approach to everyday life:** How can you be more intentional with your time? List five things you can change to maximize the hours you have every day.

❏ **Assess the nonnegotiables your leadership role requires:** Such negotiables may deadlines, your character, and equipping others to lead. Adjust how you schedule your time accordingly.

❏ **Incorporate a specific plan of action:** Enlist help, remove unnecessary activities, get time management training, and anticipate obstacles.

❏ **Stay focused:** Match your priorities and activities with your goals and values. The changes you make must be in line with these goals and values.

Read Psalm 31:15a to see how we are to regard the use of our time.

DECLUTTER!

A popular home-and-garden TV network features several series that demonstrate the importance of homeowners' decluttering their houses before trying to sell them. The homeowners often find it hard to see past the clutter they have learned to live with—too much furniture, crowded closets, piles of books, shelves stuffed with knickknacks, counters topped with every small appliance known to man, baskets of laundry, and so on. So the buyer can see the best features of a seller's home, the hosts of these shows all say, "Declutter! Put everything you can in a storage facility."

Clutter is confusing and distracting. Could the same thing be said about the day-to-day clutter of our busy lives? Of course. Our bedrooms are cluttered, and our kitchen sinks are full of dirty dishes. In the garage we have to step over boxes and lawn equipment. Our cars are filled with fast-food sacks, old coffee cups, and yesterday's soccer socks. At work, the community center, or even church for a planning meeting, we lift our heavy, overflowing totes and struggle through the door hoping we aren't late—again!

The suggestion to declutter your life is not a new one. We've been hearing it for years, and yet a lot of us haven't taken the steps to make it happen. Recently, I decluttered the counters in our kitchen. Over time, I added fruit and vegetable containers, a coffee maker, and a toaster. Soon, snacks were left out. A new clock had a place along with a few decorative pieces. Put it all together, and it was simply too much. Now, we are still trying to find some of the things that were previously out in the open. The counters are beautiful (now that we can see them again), and I love the new feel of the room. Decluttering never ends, does it? While I don't do much cooking, I'll admit I like the cleaner look!

Like my kitchen, our lives become cluttered with letters, Post-its, and magazines. All this clutter interferes with organizing and planning. How many times a day do you hunt for a misplaced email or letter? Clutter in our lives, both personal and professional, hinders us from doing our best.

Perhaps our greatest failure regarding time management is that nasty word *procrastination*. We all procrastinate; it's just a matter of *when* not *if*! Why? There are at least three reasons. First, we justify our lack of action because the task is unpleasant. Who really wants to clean the kitchen floor? It's like the plaque I saw the other day in a craft store: *Wash, Dry, Fold, Repeat*. Isn't that the truth about a lot of things we do? You want to put making the call to the complaining customer at the bottom of your list. Since we don't like possible confrontations, we wait until the last minute to get approval for a women's event at church. We put off enlisting volunteers for the community event. Procrastination undermines our effectiveness as leaders.

Second, we procrastinate because deep down, we are afraid of failure. The risks just seem too high. Perhaps you are new in a supervisory position and are uncertain about launching a mandated training program, so you procrastinate. What will your boss say if you do it wrong? A leader of volunteers has the added concern that no one will come. Negativity and uncertainty undermine our efforts before we even start!

Third, we don't know where to begin. This could be because you are unprepared for the task. To properly organize an event, you need a solid foundation of knowledge before you begin making to-do lists. Anticipate the questions people may ask and the problems your teams may encounter beforehand, and work from that point. I find it helps to work backward from the deadline date. Review your timeline and lists regularly so you have a clear idea of how things are progressing.

DO THIS ONE THING

To help you see how you use your time, keep a log of your activities for four days in 15-minute segments. This will reveal a lot about how you value your time.

Consider the cost of your time. Is that new furniture or vacation worth the overtime? The satisfaction you feel for working on the prom committee requires 20 hours away from your family. Is that a good way to spend your time? We will do well to remember 1 Corinthians 14:40 (ESV), "But all things should be done decently and in order."

PARTS OF THE WHOLE

Leaders who want to be efficient time managers must give attention to several other related areas. Women of all ages and different backgrounds are interested in being focused, having strong visions, goal setting, and becoming more organized. Nothing positive will happen in any of these areas if a leader does not manage her time well. Time is like an umbrella over everything a leader attempts to do. Show me a leader who uses her time to the max, and I'll be looking at a woman who is focused, goal-oriented, and organized.

I SEE THE TREES *AND* THE FOREST!

A leader's focus can make or break her effectiveness. One question on my women's leadership survey was, "How do you stay focused on doing what the Lord is leading you to do and not let yourself get in the way?" Once a leader determines her call, the next step is to stay focused to accomplish the details related to that call. Turn your attention to what others (the trees) need, what you should do to help develop them, and how you can encourage their creativity. It is your responsibility to see the larger picture (the forest) and predict how actions and procedures will impact the future of the group, team, or organization. Leaders should focus on strengths, rather than weaknesses.

In his book, *Managing the Non-Profit Organization*, Peter F. Drucker interviews Roxanne Spitzer-Lehmann, who, at the time, was corporate vice president for a major health care system. She had this to say about the importance of remaining focused, "If you don't know the mission, you shouldn't be around." If you struggle to stay focused, you have lots of company! A leader's sense of values should impact her daily life. A well-developed value system will help a leader filter out the activities that might be acceptable and doable but are not the best course of action for her. With these filters in place a leader won't struggle with decisions about whether to pass on an activity that won't help her build strong teams and reach goals. A leader will never reach individual or corporate goals or develop effective leaders if she has no sustaining vision and cannot remain focused.

DREAMS OR PLANS?

Do you agree with the idea that if a leader doesn't have a plan, she is just wishing? When you sit down to set goals for your new project at church, how do you balance your heart and head? Do you get carried away with grandiose plans and then realize none of them are realistic? (Hopefully, you find this out before you start.) It is almost always more fun to dive into an activity or challenge than to sit down and consider the goal (outcome) of the project. I love doing much more than strategizing! The time spent developing a solid plan of action, gathering resources, enlisting others to help, and setting deadlines is critical to the success of projects, task forces, committees, teams, activities, and events. Even the smallest assignment warrants taking the time to review its purpose, analyze its parts, and determine a course of action.

When a leader accepts an assignment (yes, I know you may not have a choice!), the first step is to settle on a course of action. Some things may be out of your control (how much money you can spend, how many can be involved, etc.), but as the leader or coordinator, it is your responsibility to define the goals of the activity and make a rough draft of how they will be reached. Leaders often must step into the unknown to fulfill their responsibilities. Many situations require a leader to find new ways of doing things because the traditional way won't work.

If you are a church missions leader, you may need to embrace new methods to involve others in missions. An outreach event might require you to examine what's happened in the past—what has worked and what has not. In other words, you may be called upon to challenge the process.

Should your leadership challenge involve developing new products, services, or methods, your plans cannot focus on the past. Rather, the plans you make and the goals you set must support your group, team, or organization's vision. I once enlisted a woman to coordinate activities for adult women within our organization. Her assignment was to develop strategies and systems to increase women's involvement at any function where adults gathered. I wanted her to inspire our organization to become involved in ministry and to lead their churches to do the same. Quite an assignment! I could almost see her creative mind at work. After several meetings with her team, she proposed a plan to present suggestions for women's involvement at every large event in our territory. Did her plan work? You bet it did! She embraced the assignment, developed a reasonable plan, and worked it out step-by-step. Her willingness to try new things moved our work with women forward in a tremendous way!

What made the plan viable was that she communicated what she wanted her team to do and provided resources so the team members could do the work. She knew what Robin Sober, a coaching consultant for the University of Michigan, said to be true, "A minute of clarification can save hours of work later." She and her team were successful because of the time she invested in planning and evaluating.

Evaluation is an important part of any successful project. What criteria can a leader use to measure success? Feedback is essential to a leader, but we don't always seek it. Face it, we are afraid of what we'll hear. Feedback, however, can help us at any stage of an event or process. People involved in previous endeavors may tell you things to avoid before you begin. In the middle of a project, it's good to know what isn't working so you can adjust before it becomes a crisis. What evaluation of an event is better than the comments of the people who attended? Asking for feedback after an event can provide valuable information. Leaders may not ask for feedback because they fear they will lose control if someone else expresses ideas to make the project or event better. We'd rather forge ahead, holding information to ourselves, rather than take the time to solicit what others think. Timing is important when seeking feedback. If you ask too early, not enough will have happened, and the results won't be in. If you wait too long, details and impressions will be forgotten. Leaders must trust the opinion and insights of others and value the honest responses that come.

If concerns are out in the open, they can only add to the success of any project. It doesn't matter if you are the leader of a Bible study group, a task force at work, or the coordinator of a yearlong volunteer program. Once feedback comes in, what do you do with it? Listen to everything first before responding. As you evaluate what others tell you, try to understand their perspective and attitude. A wise leader never gets defensive. She never takes negative feedback personally. If others' responses surprise you, step back and reevaluate your plans before continuing.

There are basically two kinds of planning: short-term and long-term, and you may use both types for a single event or project. When you set a timeline, there are short-term plans you need to make before launching long-term details. Here are some examples of things you need to do immediately: enlist volunteers; contact speakers, musicians, seminar leaders, etc.; and make meeting space arrangements. Even though these are part of the whole, they cannot be relegated to a lower place on the to-do list than their importance dictates. It can be easy to concentrate on catchy seminar titles, eye-catching publicity, state-of-the-art decorations, tasty meals, and comfortable housing arrangements and neglect key elements. That's when the nightmares begin! Last minute decisions often create poor quality results. It's a disaster waiting to happen!

If you are coordinating volunteers for a community fundraiser, it may be necessary to have multiple planning sessions. You, as leader, however, must have a larger scope—a plan for the entire event. If your subcommittees overspend, whose responsibility will that be? Yours! If the publicity goes out late, who is responsible? You! Make a plan, and work the plan.

Creator of the iconic books about Winnie-the-Pooh, A. A. Milne, said, "Organization is what you do before you do something, so that when you do it, it is not all mixed up." Profound statement, right? If what Milne said is true, why do we get it so wrong so often? The answer to this question is that we aren't intentional about how we use our days. When we don't plan each day, the 24 hours fly by, and we realize we haven't accomplished much—and none of what we really needed to do. What can be done to stop this waste? We must realize that once a day is gone, it is irretrievable. Asked what the most surprising thing about life was, Billy Graham responded, "The brevity of it."

Effective leaders realize that not only are their to-do lists important, but the timeframes within which they work are also limited. There isn't a lot of time for do-overs. Make informed decisions to prioritize your time for maximum effect. This doesn't happen automatically—there must be organization. Have you ever been a member of a small group that seemed to function on the fly? Or have you attended meetings where there was no agenda, the leader arrived late, and the meeting space wasn't set up? No one likes to be part of a floundering group. Too many efforts are doomed to failure because of a leader's failure to organize.

What about you as a leader? Will your failure to organize affect what you do as a leader? Of course it will!

WHAT COMES FIRST?

Good leaders organize their thoughts before embarking on making timelines or detailed plans. For the moment, let's consider planning a large event for women in your organization. You are the primary coordinator; in other words, every buck stops with you. Follow my train of thought as we walk through the organizational stages to make the event successful and motivational.

1. Determine the purpose of the event. Is your event inspirational, motivational, or educational?

2. Other than attendance, what are the secondary goals of the event?

3. Allot a budget for the event, and divide the total amount into sections related to the event (i.e., publicity, décor, gifts, honorariums, housing, etc.).

4. Choose a theme. Your team may help with this, but the leader should have several possibilities in mind ahead of time to facilitate brainstorming.

While you may assign tasks to subcommittees, the list above needs to be the guiding document. Remember, the buck stops with you. When the event is over and you are justifying its viability, you must be able to point to an organized effort.

KEEP MOVING

Now that you have a solid, organized beginning, it's time to call your sub-committee leaders together for intense planning. Ready for another list? Here are things to consider as you make detailed plans for a successful event.

1. Divide the organizing details by topic and assign a team member to coordinate everything that relates to it. For example, registration, seminar hostesses, greeters, hospitality gifts, speaker, musician, host, project leaders, stage décor, and other decorations.

2. Reserve critical budgetary items for yourself. Hotel contracts, meal arrangements, publicity, and honorariums should always be handled by the primary leader. Financial responsibility lies squarely in the leader's lap. (Note: I once served on a team where the leader asked the newest member to handle all the finances for the upcoming annual event. You can imagine how that turned out!)

3. Be certain everyone on the team has a responsibility. Set report deadlines, and make your expectations clear.

4. Communicate clearly and frequently. As the leader, it is your responsibility to be sure all the threads of the event come together.

5. Depending on the event, you may set monthly and weekly deadlines to help the subcommittees stay current with their assignments. Again, you will be the master detailer as you keep careful watch over everyone's progress.

6. Every leader needs a dependable assistant. Choose this person carefully. Whoever fills this role must work closely with you and be able to take initiative when necessary.

Let me give you an example of the importance of the last item on this list. The night before our major event, my brother called to say my father was in the hospital. My mother was with me at the event, so I had to get both of us to the hospital. Because I obsess with organization at times, I had made a huge notebook with every event detail. All the seminar outlines and copies of the handouts, schedules, speaker introductions, and all assignments were there. I called my assistant for the event and presented her with the notebook. She and the leadership team ran the event smoothly—even though I wasn't there. Not only was she a capable assistant but she had also become an excellent leader herself.

WHY ALL THE FUSS ABOUT ORGANIZATION?

When a leader takes the time to plan her day, she will be rewarded not only with a work accomplished but also by the satisfaction of having done her best. It all comes down to this: if you have no plan and are not organized, you will not reach your leadership potential. Sounds simple, doesn't it?

A leader who is focused will be interested in establishing priorities to help make decisions about her work. If you direct a children's choir, what are your priorities? To teach children the joy of music? To show them music can enrich their lives? Or to keep them occupied for an hour each week? Maybe you lead a women's support group. What's the main message you want them to hear? There is help for them? God loves them? The group is a safe place? It comes down to priorities, and priorities are set by the leaders. A strong decision-maker is a desirable leader.

An indecisive person is not usually the person you want launching a new ministry. All of us make poor decisions. Can you name any Bible characters who were poor decision makers? How about Eve? David? Saul? Aaron? Solomon? John Mark? Oh, then there's Peter! Leaders don't always make the right decisions, but if we think through the processes and establish filters, we will have a higher rate of success in making the right choices.

✓ **Study the issue** before making a decision.

✓ **Gather facts** to help you make a sound decision.

✓ **Listen** to what others are saying (not to sway you but to give perspective and information).

✓ **Narrow your options.** What works in one situation may not work in another.

✓ **Compare your convictions with possible decisions.** If they don't match, discard them.

✓ **Once you've done this work, pray for God's wisdom.** Remember Jesus prayed the entire night before He selected the 12 apostles (Luke 6:12–16).

✓ **Make the decision.**

✓ **Follow through.**

> If you're not careful with the decisions you make in your life and career, you'll eventually be known for those actions—even if you don't think they're the truest indicator of who you really are.
> —ILAN MOCHARI, *INC.COM*

Pay Dirt

So, it's just a matter of time, isn't it? If leaders use their time effectively, stay focused, set goals, and get organized, will they be successful? It's not a guarantee, but these learned skills can set a leader on the path to becoming a strong, reliable individual others will respect and follow. Notice I used the term *learned skills*. This is an important distinction. A person can develop her abilities in these four areas and thereby increase her ability to help others learn, grow, and become a good leader.

---◆---

How important are integrity and values in a leader's life?

Can a leader experience joy in her leading?

When news about the arrests was announced, residents of the small town were astounded. How could something like this happen in their little city? Surely the accused hadn't thought they would get away with embezzling $42 million! As the media revealed more about the situation, townspeople found city officials, including a former police chief and city manager, were among those facing criminal charges and prison. Everyone accused was viewed as a leader in their community. Although extreme, this is a perfect example of how leaders can abuse their authority and destroy their trust and influence. The thieves put personal gain ahead of the community's well being and lived in extreme comfort for many years before their illegal actions were uncovered. These individuals had twisted values, and integrity was lost in a mire of distorted justifications.

This chapter will focus on three more areas about which participants of my women's leadership survey were curious. The surveys indicated followers desired to know their leaders more personally, and the questions posed focused on values, integrity, and the joys of leadership.

There is a progression or logic, if you will, to these three areas. If a leader has a well-defined system of values, her actions will reflect the choices she has already made. Her decision-making process is sensitive to the needs and interests of others. Her strategies are determined by her beliefs about ethical behavior, loyalty, and attitude and create a lifestyle that is a daily testimony to what she is convicted is right and honorable. A leader's values lead to integrity, and out of that comes joy from our work. After the dust settles on leadership challenges, and the dark days of struggle have past, what remains is joy and the knowledge of having done one's best.

Before discussing values, integrity, and the joys of leadership, let's review what Proverbs 16:10–20 (*The Message*) tells us about how we are to lead. Whether you have an elected position or serve as a volunteer at the local library, your responsibilities for honorable leading are the same. This passage is replete with leadership principles that still have meaning for us today. Spend a few minutes reading about God's instructions to leaders. There are key concepts you should find in this passage:

✦ "A good leader . . . doesn't exploit" (v. 10)—Does this mean leaders should not take advantage of followers? Exploitation such as misappropriation of funds? Or using power for personal advantage?

✦ "Honesty in the workplace" (v. 11)—Truthfulness? Promise-making?

✦ "Sound leadership has a moral foundation" (v. 12)—Do others see that your spiritual foundation dictates your choices, behavior, and worldview?

✦ "Good leaders cultivate honest speech" (v. 13)—Can others believe what you say? Leaders must create a climate of trust and honest communication.

✦ "An intemperate leader wreaks havoc in lives" (v. 14)—Do others see that you maintain a sense of self-discipline and personal responsibility?

✦ "Good-tempered leaders invigorate lives; they're like spring rain and sunshine" (v. 15)—Are you a leader who refreshes others, or does your ego cause trouble?

✦ "It pays to take life seriously; things work out when you trust in GOD." (v. 20)—Can those trust your leadership due to your commitment to God's direction and self-control?

The day I started writing this chapter, I was in one of my favorite Starbucks cafés in Louisville, Kentucky. I was standing in line when the woman in front of me greeted a co-worker in line behind me. They talked over and around me about a recent push for performance to reach a large goal at work. Both were excited about the results. He asked, "I wonder why we made the goal this time?" She replied, "Well, there was a synergy, an enthusiasm we hadn't had before. And, it was just purposeful, you know?" He nodded his head (I fought the urge to nod too!) and said, "You know, *purposeful* is the right word. What do think made the difference?" She said, "I hate to say it, but it was leadership. It was leadership that made the difference." Had there been a shake-up in corporate structure? Short of interrupting their conversation, I'll never know for sure.

Can you believe I overheard this right there in Starbucks? So, leaders *do* make a difference when they are committed, passionate, and enthusiastic. The results are strong because a leader has a clear vision and is able to motivate others to action.

VAL·UE \ˈVAL-(ˌ)YÜ\

The values one holds serve as a broad guideline in all situations. Therefore, a leader's life should be lived according to a system of beliefs. If a preschool teacher believes every young life is precious, she'll demonstrate that in the loving way she teaches. A Christian leader in the workplace may be challenged concerning the value she places on honesty, and she may find herself reprimanded for not being part of the team.

Regardless of the responsibilities you have as a leader, values are a critical element in how you approach work, relationships, and personal life decisions. There have been a lot of discussions surrounding how women function in the workplace. As I've talked with women about their work in the past 30 years, they have told me that honesty and respect for others is important, especially in the workplace. They value empathy, patience, and flexibility in their leaders and co-workers as well as leaders being direct with their employees.

CHOOSING WHAT YOU VALUE

If set values are to be a leader's standard, it follows that they must be chosen carefully. If a leader makes the choice to live by the values she was taught, they can continue to be guiding principles. Following is a list of things you may incorporate into your life to help you make strong decisions, create stable relationships, develop an honest work ethic, or deal with people. Put a checkmark next to the ones that influence your life.

❑ Accountability   ❑ Faith
❑ Achievement   ❑ Fidelity
❑ Assertiveness   ❑ Grace
❑ Balance   ❑ Growth
❑ Clear-mindedness   ❑ Joy
❑ Commitment   ❑ Obedience
❑ Compassion   ❑ Preparation
❑ Dependability   ❑ Righteousness
❑ Efficiency   ❑ Serenity
❑ Enthusiasm   ❑ Temperance
❑ Excellence   ❑ Trustworthiness
❑ Fairness   ❑ Vision

I've learned a lot from Pastor Jack Hayford. In his book *Appointed to Leadership: God's Principles for Spiritual Leaders,* he outlines how Christians are to lead, and it starts with your own personals values. Values influence a leader's approach to her leadership responsibilities as she seeks to be a stable spiritual leader. Think about the following ways you can lead under God's direction and influence others:

✦ Walk with God daily, which requires an intimate relationship with Him.
✦ Focus on God's call for leading, and strive for excellence in all you do.
✦ Personify God's love as you work with others.
✦ Share that your abilities and skills are blessings from God.
✦ Rely on the Holy Spirit's guidance for your ministry.
✦ Study God's Word for direction as a leader.

As you develop or reaffirm your system of values, what should be your guiding standard? God's Word is the ultimate instruction manual. Our behavior, attitude, relationships, outlook on life, view of eternity, and our position with Christ are all influenced by what we value most. After you make your personal list of values, prioritize the top ones and review them. Can you verbalize why you hold them in high esteem? Do they represent the things you would support, even if it isn't popular? Many decisions a leader makes are a reflection of what she most values.

Have you considered how comforting it can be to rely on your values? You can use your values as a strong guiding force to help you choose the right direction. A new career? Engaging in a ministry in your church? Faced with a dilemma at work? You've chosen values with meaning to you; now use them to help you be a more effective leader.

> Leave no questioning in anyone's mind as to where you stand.
>
> —ANONYMOUS

IN·TEG·RI·TY \IN-'TE-GRƏ-TĒ\

The word *integrity* is synonymous with honesty, morality, virtue, and truthfulness, and the dictionary defines it as "the quality of being honest and fair, the state of being complete or whole." This definition refers to a person having a moral compass that has become a personality trait. Wouldn't we all like to have others use this word to describe us?

It's no surprise then, that integrity is highly regarded in the Bible. Look up the following verses to see how God views those who are honest and upright in their dealings with others: Psalm 41:12; Proverbs 11:3; 12:22; 21:3; 28:6; 29:2; Philippians 4:8; Hebrews 13:18

To be known as a person of integrity means you are an influencer, whether you set out to be one or not. In order to lead, leaders must want to influence others. Politicians stir people to vote for them. Evangelists influence individuals to accept Christ as their Savior. Teachers motivate their students to learn. Doctors want their patients to live healthier lives. Motivational speakers spur others to action. If a a leader lacks commitment, loyalty, or honesty, these traits will come out at some point, and followers will fall away. I am always amazed during election years that leaders assume their past behavior won't come to light under the scrutiny of the media. A leader's integrity, or lack of, will *not* go unnoticed!

> Live your life in such a way that you wouldn't be afraid to sell the family parrot to the town gossip.
>
> —WILL ROGERS

BEING AN INFLUENCER

There are several things a leader can do to ensure that her influence is positive. Colossians 3:23 (*The Message*) says, "Do your best. Work from the heart for your real Master." A leader who wants to have influence must work wholeheartedly and strive for excellence in everything. When leaders work for God, an entirely new dimension slips into place. Influencing others requires being single-minded. Knowing there is no guarantee of extended days or weeks should cause a leader to focus. James 4:14 (*The Message*) speaks to the fleeting nature of life: "You don't know the first thing about tomorrow. You're nothing but a wisp of fog, catching a brief bit of sun before disappearing."

So, what's the result of integrity? Influence! Here's a list of characteristics that John Maxwell says, in his book *Leadership Gold*, we need in order to be a candidate for influence:

✦ Insight: *What you know*
✦ Ability: *What you do*
✦ Character: *Who you are*
✦ Passion: *What you feel*
✦ Success: *What you achieve*
✦ Intuition: *What you sense*
✦ Confidence: *How secure you make others feel*
✦ Charisma: *How you connect*

He concludes by saying, *"If you embody these characteristics, your influence will increase."*

CAN A LEADER EXPERIENCE JOY IN LEADING?

Several survey participants asked, "What brings you joy?"

The Bible is not silent about joy. Read the following verses in different versions, and memorize your favorite to comfort you during challenging leadership situations. These verses explain not only the reason for joy but remind us to look for joy in every circumstance. Every leader has experienced times when it is difficult to find joy. Attitudes are negative, finances are dismal, relationships are damaged, and communication is nonexistent. It's hard to find joy when your boss is unhappy with your team's performance or when your special project is given to someone else.

> *Consider it a sheer gift, friends, when tests and challenges come at you from all sides.*
> —JAMES 1:2 *THE MESSAGE*

The joy of GOD is your strength!

—NEHEMIAH 8:10 *THE MESSAGE*

God's kingdom isn't a matter of what you put in your stomach, for goodness' sake. It's what God does with your life as he sets it right, puts it together, and completes it with joy.

—ROMANS 14:17 *THE MESSAGE*

DO THIS ONE THING

Think about a time when you found a silver lining during a difficult or tense leadership situation. Write down the situation and then the positive things you discovered.

Situation: _____

_____

_____

_____

_____

Silver lining I discovered: _____

_____

_____

_____

_____

HOW IMPORTANT ARE INTEGRITY AND VALUES IN A LEADER'S LIFE?
CAN A LEADER EXPERIENCE JOY IN HER LEADING?

Situation: _____

_____

_____

_____

_____

Silver lining I discovered: _____

_____

_____

_____

_____

Situation: _____

_____

_____

_____

_____

Silver lining I discovered: _____

_____

_____

_____

_____

Now, think about a current situation . . . can you find a silver lining?

———————

All leaders have stories to tell about their experiences! It's tempting to wallow in the negative aspects of some of those experiences. On the other hand, when we can recall the humorous or the unusual situations, we can "count it all joy" (James 1:2 KJV).

Several years ago I addressed a church missions committee about how they could lead their church membership to participate more in missions. The group was receptive to my comments, and I felt my investment of time was well spent. When I spoke at a luncheon for the church's women the next day, a girl came up and asked to talk. She had been at the committee meeting the day before, so I was surprised when she said she was only 14 years old. She said, "What you said yesterday and today showed me that God wants me to be involved in missions. I don't know how yet, but I'm going to start doing things and see what He wants me to do." Her comments were refreshing, and again I felt my travel and preparation time had been worth it. But that's not the end of the story! Two years later a young woman spoke to me at an event and asked me if I remembered her. One look at her name tag was all I needed. She had been active in local missions, gone on an international missions trip, and was still interested in seeing how God would lead her. The joys of leadership come from all ages!

My daughter's first missions leader placed herself in my path one weekend in Nevada. I hadn't seen her since my daughter Janna was in the second grade! She had served on a regional missions team I had led, and I had mentored her about 18 years before when I lived in Denver. She was still involved in leading missions groups and thanked me for all I'd taught her. The joys of leadership will continue to come—even though many years pass!

Likewise, the joys of leadership often come when we least expect them. A number of years ago, I worked with two distinctly different groups of women. One group was cooperative, but the other was not! Not only that, but they believed their responsibilities conflicted and were in opposition to the other group's role. What a tough leadership challenge! As skillfully as I could, I worked to bring their differing purposes and structures under one umbrella. Talk about sleepless nights! And many prayer sessions too.

I was coordinating a women's event when the leaders of the two groups came to me before we began a worship session. They asked if they could they speak to me. *Now?* I thought. "We need to settle something right now." *Oh no! This doesn't sound good!* Numbly, I nodded and waited for them to share their news. To my surprise, their news was that they couldn't see any value in remaining two separate groups. They believed their purposes, rather than being in conflict, actually complemented one another. They realized they would have more influence working together. Can you imagine how excited I was?

WHAT DO I DO WHEN I CAN'T FIND JOY IN LEADERSHIP?

When you have trouble finding the silver linings of leadership, there may be several dynamics at work in your life. Your joy in leading will be limited if . . .

1. You are suffering from burnout. Feeling overwhelmed or underappreciated will cause you to second-guess decisions, harm your interactions with others, and damage your influence.

2. You are not authentic. Others can spot counterfeit leaders a mile away! If you present a phony persona, people won't trust you. Leaders must be genuine in their care for their team members. Bogus claims, false pretenses, and pseudoenthusiasm undermine a leader's ability to achieve positive long-term results.

3. You are stressed or frustrated. Remaining calm in difficult circumstances cannot be underestimated. No one wants to follow a leader

who can't manage stress and gives in to the challenges and vexations of leadership responsibilities.

4. You are unprepared. Leaders must be lifelong learners. How long has it been since you've taken a leadership seminar or read a book on leadership? If you want to discover the joy of leadership, keep your leadership skills sharp.

5. You don't have a personal relationship with Jesus. Look back over your life and see where God's hand has led you. Allow time to study His Word and hear His voice. If you don't have Christ as your personal Savior, read the following verses to help you understand how to invite Him into your life: Romans 3:23 and 10:9–10; Revelation 22:17.

> *Oh! May the God of green hope fill you up with joy, fill you up with peace, so that your believing lives, filled with the life-giving energy of the Holy Spirit, will brim over with hope!*
> —ROMANS 15:13 *THE MESSAGE*

Pay Dirt

When leaders have values that come from a heartfelt study of God's Word, they will live with integrity. The reward of such purposeful living will be a multitude of leadership joys that are expected, unforeseen, and amazing!

CHAPTER 11

Personal Thoughts about Leadership

Some of the questions asked on the women's leadership survey were asked of me personally. At the time, I held a demanding leadership role within a Christian denominational structure and maintained a heavy travel schedule. My participation in meetings, seminars, and retreats required an intense amount of preparation time and lots of interaction with people. I was frequently asked how I balanced all the activities, so I've saved these questions directed to me for this last chapter. Maybe one of them will be exactly what you need. I hope my answers that follow will help you make sound decisions and filter through sticky situations you are encountering in your leadership life.

Please note these answers are my personal opinions, not responses based on research or on anyone else's ideas.

How does Jesus guide you on a daily basis?
Because I believe the Bible has all the answers I need to every situation, it is the first source I use as I chart my course of action and how to relate to others. I believe while the exact word or situation may not be specifically named, *every* answer to *every* question about how we as Christians should respond to others or behave can be found in God's Word. God speaks to me through His Word, and then I pray for final, confirmed guidance. In my current leadership roles, I maintain what I call filters, which are my priorities, directions, and strategy. (For more on this read

chapters 3, 8, 9.) As situations arise, I don't spend much time on a decision because I have already made it prior to its appearance. That saves a lot of time and frustration and enables me to move forward more quickly. It may look as if I move full steam ahead with little thought, but actually, I have spent study time in advance about various contingencies that may come my way. With predetermined priorities I can decide with certainty that I am within God's will. My convictions about honesty, integrity, how I treat others, consistency, and the purpose of my leadership role dictate what plans I make and what activities I choose.

What Bible verses or passages do you lean on the most?
There are three verses that mean a lot to me. Habakkuk 1:5, "Look at the nations and watch—and be utterly amazed. For I am going to do something in your days that you would not believe, even if you were told." As both a Christian and a leader it is encouraging to know that God wants to work through me. The amazing things He has planned would boggle our minds if we knew about them in advance. Even if we did know, we wouldn't believe them, would we? Our plans are too small; God's plans are big and perfect. We do not know what's ahead of us, while nothing surprises God! I can't count the number of times when the plans I made changed and God still used the glitches, the mistakes, and the incompletes for His glory.

Second Corinthians 8:12 (*The Message*) is another favorite verse: "Once the commitment is clear, you do what you can, not what you can't. The heart regulates the hands." I adopted this verse to guide my personal involvement in ministry. My personality leans toward a lot of activity! My father once asked me, "Don't you ever just sit still?" He'd been watching me talk as I watched television with one eye and crocheted a baby blanket with the other. I have to be careful that my tendency to constant activity doesn't lead to meaningless movement. While I want to be productive, I want my activities to be within what God wants me to do. I enjoy involvement in a wide variety of ministries because another part of my personality loves doing new things. I've painted houses in Mexico, taught women in Croatia how to become leaders, led missions studies, planned women's events, and made sandwiches for inner-city homeless. Like anyone else—I tend to change ministries with the seasons. Cold weather brings thoughts of hats and gloves for the homeless while the holidays bring to mind food baskets for the needy. Gifts for children are an annual need that never changes. Spring and summer bring ideas for ministries with children: Vacation Bible School, neighborhood parties, and missions camps. Sometimes when I read 2 Corinthians 8:12, I read it with joy because of the blessings I've received from ministering to others. Unfortunately, at other times, I look at my hands only to discover they have been empty for a week, maybe two. What does that say about my heart?

My favorite verse is Jeremiah 29:11: "'For I know the plans I have for you,' declares the LORD, 'plans to prosper you and not to harm you, plans to give you hope and a future.'" This verse, more than any other perhaps, calms me and directs my perspective. When difficulties arise or situations become too complicated, this verse comes to my mind, and I realize once again that God is truly in control of my life and what happens around me. Knowing that the final outcome is in Another's hands reassures me that as long as I move within His perfect will and seek Him, I am never outside His protection. It doesn't mean my life will be smooth, but it does mean I am never alone. As a leader I can hide under God's wings and lean on Him to guide me as I work to mentor others, develop my skills, and accomplish the tasks assigned to me as a leader.

What is the most important leadership skill?

A radio interviewer asked this same question when we discussed my book *5 Leadership Essentials for Women*. As I've completed extensive research on leadership development, I am convinced that if a woman wants to be an effective leader, she must develop her communication skills. If she fails to be clear in her communication (written or spoken), she will find herself in situations fraught with hurt feelings, angry recriminations, and irritated people! This particular leadership skill is too important to be left to chance. Sending memos, emails, or text messages does not mean communication has taken place. Every report needs to be analyzed, every email reread for errors, and every verbal interchange inspected for potential misunderstandings.

There is a wealth of books on how to become a good communicator. One of my favorites is *How to Say It for Women* by Dr. Phyllis Mindell. In it, Mindell gives specific examples of ways women diminish the power of their communication, and the challenges readers to assess what they say and how they say it. Each chapter has practice sections to help readers apply what they've read.

Your followers expect you to keep them informed and remind them of the purpose and challenges facing your organization. It's through open communication (led by you as the leader) that your group will reach its goals. When we fail to make ourselves understood or remain aloof from members, we create a cloud of confusion, damage relationships, and discourage participation. I don't know about you, but I'm not too interested in joining a group in which the leader is removed and uncommunicative. A leader cannot stay in the background. That's often a cover for laziness! An effective leader doesn't approach her tasks with the "If they are interested and committed, they'll ask" attitude. I would suggest several things to help you grow as a communicator:

✓ **When in doubt, communicate.** It's better for your group to get several well-informed emails than to be left guessing.

✓ **Be thorough in what you say.** Once you've written your communication, reread it to insure it covers the basic information followers need to complete their assignments. If it helps, make a list of the details, and check them off as you list them in the written piece.

✓ **Follow-up is critical in communicating!** Restate what you've said. Clearly identify your main points for the reader.

✓ **Ask for a response.** This ensures two things: they received the communication, and you know they have read it. Establish firm and recognizable deadlines. Don't hide deadlines; make them clear. If you do not receive a reply, send a "second request for information" message.

✓ **When in doubt about anything you've said or written, communicate again.**

Can you name the leadership qualities you learned from a leadership mentor?

When I assumed the most challenging leadership position I've ever had, I looked to an older woman who had many years of experience. She had been serving as a volunteer for months, and I realized she had things to tell me. She was a positive woman, and I knew I could trust her observations and suggestions. That kind of trust in a mentor is critical because the information you need should come from a person with integrity and credibility. She taught me to be myself and to refine my plans and actions with God's help. Through her wisdom and guidance she encouraged me to move forward in developing a strategy for my work once I had the facts I needed to make informed decisions. By her example she confirmed the value of being organized and having a strong work ethic. This woman knew how to mentor others! Her experience taught me more than I could have ever learned from how-to books. Her leadership positions had taken her down roads most women never traveled, and I benefited from her hard-earned knowledge. She told me two things I'll never forget: "Don't be afraid to take risks! Be creative." And, "If you don't take care of yourself, no one else will!" That's one reason I learned how to schedule times of relaxation into my busy schedule.

How do you prepare to lead?

Preparation to lead comes in many forms. When I begin a new leadership position, I learn the requirements and how things were done in the past. I gather as much information as I can about people's expectations. By reading old reports and talking to people in the group or organization, I may hear negative comments and encounter criticism, but that's all right because it gives me a broader picture of the situation. It was hard not to go in and begin making changes I was sure needed to be made. But instead, I gathered information, read, studied, and then with those I enlisted to help, I initiated new methods and creative processes to accomplish our task.

I want a written, detailed job description of my duties. I am adamant about telling people under me what I expect of them. The next step is to determine my priorities. If the organization or employer has set goals, studying these well help set your priorities. Your priorities should be in line with and support the organization's priorities.

What others think about my priorities may just be their own ideas and may not help me lead. Not that I don't consider others' opinions, but the specifics laid out by the organization determine my priorities. The "how" may be different from my predecessor's, but that's OK because no two leaders are the same. With a list of priorities, I present them to my employer, supervisor, or chairperson to make sure I correctly understand the objective.

When the overall structure, strategy, or scheme is set, I make specific, detailed plans. I'm a list-maker, so here come the lists! I categorize the "Need to Do" and the "Must Do" items. If necessary, I set deadlines, and I make a list of questions. With quasi plans made, I move to the team, group, or organization for presentation. For me, the lists never go away; they just evolve into new ones!

How do you study?

I developed my personal process for preparation in high school and college. (I think I inherited the organization gene from my father!) Now, when I face a busy speaking schedule, the first thing I do is make a list of all the upcoming dates. I list the date, the event, my responsibility, the seminar title or speaker's theme, and the time allotment. Once that list is complete, I keep a copy in a file on my laptop and a print copy in my tote bag that goes nearly everywhere with me. Then I begin to gather materials I'll need to prepare myself. That may be in book form, online research, or magazine articles. I prepare a file for each engagement or event and arrange my research in my desk filing drawer by date so everything is at my fingertips. I go through my own resources and file them for easy reference. Starting with the nearest speaking engagement, I work my way through information that will help me construct speeches and conferences. I have several favorite Bible reference resources, and I comb these for specific verses I may want to use as the biblical base for speaking and leading seminars. Working online is valuable during this step of my study process as I can delve deeper into a passage than my meager resources allow.

Now, this next step is something I always try to do. I work far in advance on speaking engagements and conferences so my ideas and thoughts can germinate. I give God time to affirm my direction or facilitate any changes. Leaving preparation until the last minute belies the word *preparation*. When I allow time to mull over my presentation content, I end up being better prepared because I can incorporate the information into my life. It also enables me to remember personal stories and experiences to use as illustrations. Now with God's direction, I'm ready to put thoughts to paper. I create a general outline and note where illustrations may be inserted. With the information in hand, it's time to compose my speech or seminar on my computer. All this preparation makes the writing process much quicker. Again, I leave the rough draft alone on my computer to allow for a germinating period and for God to speak to my heart. My notes aren't even printed until I review the presentation. Once I print my completed speech, I file the printed sheets in the appropriate file folder to which I add handouts and small-group activities. I make one final list of supplies I'll need for a display so that nothing is forgotten.

The real study comes after I've printed my notes. During the week of the actual event or presentation, I spend time every day reading, reviewing, and fine-tuning what I've written. I become familiar with the stories I want to tell and make sure the presentation is within my time allotment. I use a highlighter for easy viewing as I speak. While I don't memorize my content, I want to know the material well enough that my delivery is natural. I will occasionally quote someone, but I don't advocate making a presentation sound like a report or treatise. If I want to be sure I say something a specific way, I type the exact words and then underline it so I don't forget the phrasing.

All of this may sound cumbersome to you, but this is the process I use to prepare for any speech I make or conference I lead. Studying has always been fun for me. I enjoy the research phase, and I like pulling different presentation methods together. It's fun to recall humorous experiences and relate them to my topic. The best result is seeing a responsive light come to people's faces as they hear what I hope are insightful comments, motivating them to lead and stirring them to action!

How do you find time to do the things you do?
Some kind people raise their eyebrows rather than tell me outright that I might be a bit obsessive about how I approach things. The one thing that helps me use my time wisely is that I am very intentional. Rarely a day passes that I don't have a plan for how I will use the next 24 hours. Even during a recent vacation I made a plan—wake up, eat breakfast, walk to the beach, take a nap, eat lunch, go back to the beach, take a nap, eat dinner, relax in the courtyard, read a little, and go to bed. It was a tough schedule, but I kept it up for ten whole days.

All this to say I am conscious of the passing hours. If there are definite time constraints for the day, I often function from a physical list. I learned years ago to group-related activities. For example, if I am out and about, I will take care of things in the same geographical area. I figure an additional stop is better than a separate trip. When getting ready to lead a seminar, I make a list, gather the items I need, and group them together for packing. I often use my guest bedroom as a staging area. There's an empty dresser drawer in that bedroom that's perfect for handouts, display items, and other printed materials. Find a place in your home, or use a box or suitcase. Containers with wheels are the best.

We have a lot of demands on our time, and it requires a master coordinator to deal with the urgent and important daily events. If you have children and are leading in some capacity at work, church, or in your community or neighborhood, you need to be organized so no one's schedule suffers. If you work outside your home, your time is consumed with commuting, working, and family priorities. Or maybe you are retired and are wondering how you ever had time to hold down a job. We fill our days, weeks, and months to overflowing with activities that speak to our interests and abilities. I would say the most critical skill a leader can develop in managing her time is being able to determine her priorities. Take an objective, look at how you delegate, and lead your team. Be intentional. Be honest. Be proactive. Use your time wisely.

How do you deal with burnout? What do you do if those under your leadership exhibit signs of burnout?

These are heavy questions! Any leader will find times when it's hard to get up in the morning. She feels like the young man who didn't want to get up to go to church one Sunday. His wife told him it was time to get up. He hid his head under his pillow and refused to move. She called again, and this time he mumbled, "Those people down there don't like me." Once more she came into the bedroom and shook his shoulder, "You're going to be late if you don't get up right now." He replied, "I don't want to!" In a stern voice she said, "You have to go. You are the pastor!" Most of us as leaders experience times when responsibilities overwhelm us, and our inner drive fades. It's during these times we need to return to God's Word and remember His call on our lives.

I'm fairly positive most of the time, and this has kept me from many seasons of burnout. They come, but it's usually when I'm tired. Lack of sleep and exercise, poor eating habits, and too many travel hours can make us negative and unresponsive. When my travel took me away from home days at a time, I learned to schedule periods of relaxation. Listen to this: If you don't plan to relax, you won't. No one else will insert relaxation time into your schedule. If I were within 30 miles of a beach, I scheduled time to park my car and listen to the surf. It could be sunny or windy, but if I could get there, I did. You may choose to pull over on your way home from work and listen to calming music. Small things like this can revive your spirit and help you deal with crazy schedules, unplanned meetings, and looming deadlines.

Helping others in your group or organization deal with burnout is important too. Plan training time to combat burnout. Know the signs of burnout so when you see it in your co-workers, you can help them through their personal struggle. Ultimately, they are still accountable, but you can perhaps shorten the time of frustration by understanding the reasons behind it and ministering to them in Jesus' name.

What have you sacrificed to be in your current leadership role?
If I had answered this question several years ago, my answer might have been different. When I was working an average of 55 hours a week, I had little time to spend with friends and no time to plant a country garden. I didn't have a pet because I was gone too much. I missed a lot of activities and events at my church due to my heavy travel schedule. There were days when I missed these things so much that I felt I was giving up a lot to fulfill my leadership responsibilities. Some days were gray with dark woe-is-me clouds. But, God's Son would remind me through prayer and Bible study that He called me to the work and would provide my every need. Suddenly, the day would brighten. I would enjoy a friend's garden instead of my own and found other people's cats to hold. I didn't sacrifice much in the overall scheme of things. That phase of my life is over. Now with more free time, I can choose which projects and leadership roles I take on. I established new ministries in my new home and have embarked on several new leadership journeys. With family close, a Bible-preaching church, and fellowship with other believers, I am content. And, I have a cat!

What is the best thing to do—take a leave of absence to care for family or continue not giving your best?
This is an interesting question especially because I faced this very issue when my father was diagnosed with Alzheimer's. At the time I lived about five hours away from my parents, traveled long hours, and was away from home more than I was there. With only one brother, he and his wife struggled to manage all of the doctor appointments and emergencies between their jobs and responsibilities. I talked with my supervisor about possible solutions. In my heart I wanted and needed to help my

family. I considered a leave of absence, but my supervisor suggested my husband and I move closer to my parents, and I could work from home. Being deployed from the corporate office worked for me because I am a self-starter and do not need a lot of supervision.

We sold our house and moved to the mobile home park where my parents lived. We stayed for seven years and shared care of my father while helping my mother manage things. When not traveling, I was on duty.

I realize solutions aren't as simple for many, but it was something God worked out for my family and me. It might help you when faced with a similar situation to make a pro and con list to determine your best course of action. Take into account these considerations: Can you function without support staff at hand? Do you have the inner drive to accomplish your tasks independently? Will you miss the camaraderie of the office? Will your deployment cause a financial burden on your employer? Is in-person communication necessary to complete your tasks? Do not assume your employer will say no. Employers are often more flexible than we think they might be. Check to see if there are provisions for family leaves of absence in place. Talk with your supervisor about options.

Joy in Leadership

I'd be less than honest if I were to say my answers to these questions will never change. That isn't the way leadership works, is it? As we grow, things that once bothered us as leaders don't seem so daunting anymore. The leadership journey changes us. We learn to survive difficult situations and grow in our capacity to face the demands of our position. Others' hidden agendas are rarely positive for us, but we can learn how to deal with them. Personality clashes are energy leaks that threaten our groups, teams, and organizations. However, we can develop patience and the ability to diffuse volatile interactions. Poor communication can destroy relationships, but our leadership expertise can restore healthy discussions.

There is no area of leadership that is without potential difficulty! As you lead, confirm your call, keep balance in your life, avoid burnout, be diligent in your preparation, consult God's Word, enlist a mentor to help you, be a lifetime learner, become an expert communicator, and honor the time God has given you. Excelling in these areas will bring you joy in leadership!

Appendix

THE AUTHOR ASKS YOU

This book has been all about asking and answering questions concerning leadership. If you aren't too weary of questions, here are some final ones I want to personally ask you as a leader. I realize your leadership responsibilities may be simple and straightforward. Or they may be complicated and burdensome. Regardless, consider these final questions. As you reflect on them, I hope your answers will move you further into the study of leadership and the joys it can bring when you are committed and prepared.

1. What is the title of the last book on leadership you've read?

2. What have you done in the last three months to develop a leadership skill?

3. What is your greatest strength as a leader?

4. What is your most obvious weakness as a leader?

5. In your current leadership roles, are you truly committed to the positions, or are you only going through the motions?

6. Can others count on you? What says they can?

7. What Scripture verse or passage inspires you to be an effective leader?

Once you've answered these questions, turn the page and begin a new chapter in your life as a leader!

MY LEADERSHIP LIST

USING THIS BOOK

While this book was written as a resource for individuals, it also can easily be used for group study. It's question-and-answer format makes it a natural fit for group study. If you want to develop new leaders, the content can also serve as your primary reference. Consider using the book in one of the following ways:

1. Small-Group Study

Decide how long you will have for the study. Small groups work best in brief sessions, so you might choose to have three or four sessions and focus on the areas you think will benefit group members the most. Subjects such as motivation, call, spiritual growth, and balance may be of special interest.

Design one- to two-hour sessions. Begin or end with a short devotion that speaks to the day's topics. (Bible studies in Proverbs and Lamentations would be great for these.) Enlist group members to lead the devotions. Use each chapter title as an idea springboard for creating an ice-breaking activity. For example, prior to a discussion of balance, lead the group in a brief balance workout. Whatever tactics you use, make your sessions interactive. Participation is important in small-group dynamics.

Personally invite people to participate in the small group, and utilize social media to seek out people you may not know or know well. Discover what resonates with your leaders and members, and adapt the content to meet their needs.

2. Leadership Retreat

Publicize the retreat well in advance, and encourage every member of your leadership team to be present. Choose a nearby facility that's reasonable in cost. Make sure every member or your team has a copy of *Around the Table*, and suggest they read it prior to the retreat.

Enlist women to tell some of the leadership stories in chapter 1. Use leadership Bible studies on Proverbs and Lamentations as devotions for two of the sessions of your retreat (one to open and one to close your retreat).

Depending on how long your retreat is, determine which subjects you will cover, and divide the presentation responsibilities for the day(s). Be creative and encourage interaction! Here are several general ideas:

✓ Use the statistics from the sidebars in this book to create a fun true-false exercise.

✓ Print some of the quotes from the book, attach to candy or a treat, and have them read aloud.

✓ Ask team members to share their most humorous leadership experiences. Keep the accounts brief, and intersperse them with book content.

✓ Distribute paper and pens, and ask those present to draw a picture of their idea of the perfect leader. They can be humorous or serious.

3. Personal Development/Mentoring Sessions

There may be individuals you are mentoring or working with individually who are unable to attend group sessions or a retreat. If that is the case, think about how you can use *Around the Table* as a one-on-one resource. After you have read the book, develop questions for each chapter, or highlight reflection exercises from the book then point them out to your mentee. Provide them with a copy of the book, and encourage them to read it and answer the questions. Discuss them in one of your mentoring sessions. Create a reading list for future discussions (see the reading list in the appendix).

Take the Develop courses through Woman's Missionary Union®. They are designed to equip women as missions leaders and with general leadership skills. Visit wmu.com/training.

LEADERSHIP ESSENTIALS

CHECKLIST FOR LEARNING LEADERS
Check the things that are challenging you in your current leadership roles.
- ❏ I have healthy working relationships with my co-workers.
- ❏ I have the skills needed to do my work.
- ❏ I can contribute to the project/job/organization.
- ❏ My job is an appropriate fit with my abilities.
- ❏ I am influencing others toward achieving our goals.
- ❏ I build people rather than use them.
- ❏ I know my greatest strengths.
- ❏ I know why I am feeling a lot of pressure.
- ❏ I have the skills to manage the changes that need to be made.

SKILLS EVERY LEADER NEEDS
1. Be an effective communicator.
2. Be able to diffuse conflict when it arises.
3. Be prepared to build a team, group, or organization.
4. Be positive in leadership relationships.
5. Be knowledgeable in establishing priorities for wise time management.

Rate your leadership skills from 1 percent to 100 percent, indicating how successful you are in these five leadership essentials.

A SHORT LIST OF THINGS LEADERS SHOULD DO
- ✓ Remember that leading is serving.
- ✓ Carefully choose those who will work with you.
- ✓ Provide training and resources.
- ✓ Help others develop their skills.
- ✓ Be honest and demand honesty in return.
- ✓ Be consistent.
- ✓ Use sound problem-solving skills.

✓ Continue to learn.
✓ Know your strengths.
✓ Learn to delegate.
✓ Be positive and approach change with enthusiasm and determination.

ONE-WORD SUBJECT GUIDE

ADDITIONAL READING

18 Minutes: Find Your Focus, Master Distraction, and Get the Right Things Done by Peter Bregman

Awaken the Leader in You: 10 Life Essentials for Women in Leadership by Linda M. Clark

5 Leadership Essentials for Women: Developing Your Ability to Make Things Happen by Linda M. Clark

Organizing Your Day: Time Management Techniques That Will Work for You by Sandra Felton

Seasons of a Leader's Life: Learning, Leading, and Leaving a Legacy by Jeff Iorg

Knit Together: Discover God's Pattern for Your Life by Debbie Macomber

Leadership Gold: Lessons I've Learned from a Lifetime of Learning by John C. Maxwell

TeamsWork: A No-Nonsense Approach for Achieving More Together by Joyce A. Mitchell

I've listed below several Bible studies and spiritual-growth books published by Woman's Missionary Union® (WMU®) and New Hope Publishers. You can go online to wmustore.com or newhopepublishers.com to see a longer listing and to order these great resources.

MyMISSION curriculum: *Refined: Being Remade in Christ; Identity: Who We Are in Jesus; myGOD: A Study on the Attributes of God; myStory: A Study on Our Relationship with God; myTopics: Faith and Doubt*

Everyday Faith; Everyday Hope; Everyday Love; Everyday Peace; Everyday Obedience by Katie Orr

Secrets to Surrender: Living Wholeheartedly by Debby Akerman

Synced: Living Connected to the Heart of Jesus by Jennifer Kennedy Dean

He Said What?! Jesus' Amazing Words to Women by Brenda Poinsett

"Face-to-Face" series: *Elizabeth and Mary; Lois and Eunice; Euodia and Syntyche; Mary and Martha; Priscilla and Aquila; Sarah, Rachel, and Hannah; Naomi and Ruth* by Janet Thompson

Deeper Still: A Woman's Study to a Closer Walk with God by Edna Ellison

OTHER NEW HOPE LEADERSHIP RESOURCES

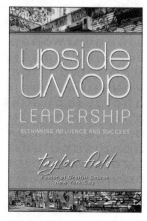

ISBN: 978-1-59669-342-5
N124147
$14.99

ISBN: 978-1-59669-211-4
N084136
$10.99

ISBN: 978-1-59669-375-3
N134116
16.99

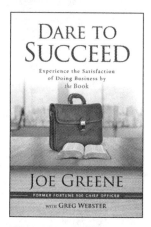

ISBN: 978-1-62591-527-6
N184101
$16.99

NEW HOPE®
PUBLISHERS
Gospel-Centered. Missions-Driven.

For more information, including where to purchase, please visit **NewHopePublishers.com**.

MORE LEADERSHIP RESOURCES

by Linda M. Clark

ISBN: 978-1-59669-431-6
N154110
$15.99

ISBN: 978-1-59669-221-3
N084144
$12.99

New Hope® Publishers is a division of WMU®, an international
organization that challenges Christian believers to understand
and be radically involved in God's mission.
For more information about WMU, go to wmu.com.
More information about New Hope books may be found at
NewHopePublishers.com. New Hope books may be
purchased at your local bookstore.

Please go to NewHopePublishers.com
for more helpful information about *Around the Table*.

If you've been blessed by this book, we would like to hear
your story. The publisher and author welcome your
comments and suggestions at: newhopereader@wmu.org.